VOICES FROM THE OTHER SIDE

VOICES FROM THE OTHER SIDE

AN ORAL HISTORY OF TERRORISM AGAINST CUBA

Keith Bolender

Introduction by Noam Chomsky

PlutoPress
www.plutobooks.com

For Magalita

Tu sabes

First published 2010 by Pluto Press
345 Archway Road, London N6 5AA and
175 Fifth Avenue, New York, NY 10010

www.plutobooks.com

Distributed in the United States of America exclusively by
Palgrave Macmillan, a division of St. Martin's Press LLC,
175 Fifth Avenue, New York, NY 10010

British Library Cataloguing in Publication Data
A catalogue record for this book is available from the British Library

ISBN   978 0 7453 3041 9   Hardback
ISBN   978 0 7453 3040 2   Paperback

Library of Congress Cataloging in Publication Data applied for

This book is printed on paper suitable for recycling and made from fully managed
and sustained forest sources. Logging, pulping and manufacturing processes are
expected to conform to the environmental standards of the country of origin.

10   9   8   7   6   5   4   3   2   1

Designed and produced for Pluto Press by
Chase Publishing Services Ltd, 33 Livonia Road, Sidmouth, EX10 9JB, England
Typeset from disk by Stanford DTP Services, Northampton, England
Printed and bound in the European Union by
CPI Antony Rowe, Chippenham and Eastbourne

Contents

Acknowledgments

A project of this type is the sum of the support and assistance of many people. It has been a long process, starting from efforts to open doors and convince those that the treatment of terrorism from the personal perspective was a worthwhile endeavor.

There are some who need to be noted for their contributions, I regret any names left out that should not have been. On the Cuban side Alicia Garcia was vital to start things off, as were others such as Jorge Timmosi, Enrique Ubieta, Ramon, Emilio, Paquito, everyone at ICAP, Editorial Jose Marti. I'd like to thank Juan Carlos at Capitan San Luis for permission to use archive photos and for supplying a large amount of background material for use of the hotel bombing photo, and to Ramón Torreira Crespo from his personal collection, to use the Costa Rican propaganda sheet in Chapter 4 and the newspaper cover of *La Coubre* explosion. And to Alejandro Robaina for the photo of José Basulto et al. All other photos, unless otherwise stated, were taken by the author.

David Castle at Pluto Press deserves special mention for his belief in the project and for providing the opportunity to see it to fruition. And thanks also to all the others at Pluto and Chase.

One cannot finish this without the support of friends and family, Lesme y Magaly, Lesmito and Fanny, Claudia, Martin, Steve, David, Sharon, Brian. Freddie and Richie, Heather and Michael. To Rose and Reg, I wish you were here. And all the rest.

There are some, however, without whose assistance this book would not have been possible. Noam Chomsky has consistently and unhesitatingly encouraged this work (giving so much of his valuable time, of which I remain appreciative, and still a little baffled by). Miguel Alvarez who opened so many doors and helped resolve many of the challenges that needed to be overcome. Raul Verrier who took the project under his wing and worked tirelessly without complaint to accomplish all that was asked.

To Heriberto Nicolas, my closest Cuban friend and my collaborator. The interpreter for the interviews, the translator of the Spanish edition of the book. The transportation, the encouragement and the person who believed in it unquestionably. The person who taught me patience will overcome all.

For all those who allowed me into their homes and their thoughts, thank you.

The opinions expressed in this book are those of the interviewees, not necessarily of the author or publisher.

Introduction

Noam Chomsky

Perhaps the most striking feature of Washington's war against Cuba since it dared to liberate itself at last in 1959 has been the frenzy with which it has been waged. Kennedy's Bay of Pigs invasion soon after taking office was authorized in an atmosphere of "hysteria," Defense Secretary Robert McNamara later testified before the Senate's Church Committee. At the first cabinet meeting after the failed invasion, the atmosphere was "almost savage," Undersecretary of State Chester Bowles reported, describing "an almost frantic reaction for an action program." The core component of the "action program" was a major terrorist war. Robert Kennedy, who was assigned the task of coordinating the massive campaign of state-directed international terrorism, repeatedly declared that overthrowing the government of Cuba was "the top priority of the United States Government—all else is secondary—no time, money, effort, or manpower is to be spared." The president himself was aware that allies "think that we're slightly demented" on the subject of Cuba, a condition that persists to the present. When Cuba was in dire straits after the collapse of the Soviet Union, liberal Democrats led by Bill Clinton tightened the noose, outflanking the Bush administration from the right, in order "to wreak havoc in Cuba" (Representative Robert Torricelli, who was point man). The extremism was of some concern to the Pentagon. The US Army War College in 1993 cautioned against the "innate emotional appeal" driving US policy-makers who saw Castro as "the embodiment of evil who must be punished for his defiance of the United States as well as for other reprehensible deeds"—though whether any of those conjured up ranked as high as "defiance of the United States" is doubtful.

The Kennedy brothers sought to bring the "terrors of the earth" to Cuba, in the words of JFK adviser and confidant historian Arthur Schlesinger. The terrorist war against Cuba peaked again in the late 1970s. The Reagan administration reacting by adding Cuba to the list of states that sponsor terror. The irony passed without notice, as did the fact that Cuba replaced Saddam Hussein, who had to be removed so that the Reaganites could provide substantial aid to their new friend. Saddam remained a favored friend until 1990, when he quickly shifted status to reincarnation of Hitler by committing a real crime, not trivial misdemeanors like slaughtering Kurds but disobeying orders, or perhaps misunderstanding them. After the US invasion of Iraq he was captured, tried, and sentenced to death—for crimes committed in 1982, the year when he was dropped from the list of states supporting terror. Again, the ironies passed unnoticed.

There was of course an official pretext for condemning Cuba as a terrorist state in 1982: Cuba was allegedly supporting Central Americans who were resisting the "war on terror" declared by the Reagan administration as it entered office—in reality, an extraordinary terrorist assault on Central Americans that claimed hundreds of thousands of lives and left much of the region in ruins, handed down in history as a grand victory of American idealism and promotion of democracy. The other standard official reason, until today, is Cuba's human rights record, a pretext that can only inspire ridicule outside of deeply indoctrinated circles, in the light of the human rights records of Washington's favored clients, not to speak of its own.

While launching his terrorist campaign, President Kennedy also sharply intensified the embargo that President Eisenhower had initiated—legitimately, high officials explained, because "The Cuban people [are] responsible for the regime" (Undersecretary of State

Douglas Dillon) and therefore must suffer hunger and deprivation for its sins. Kennedy agreed that it was Washington's right and duty to cause "rising discomfort among hungry Cubans." Eisenhower State Department official Lester Mallory had outlined the basic thinking in April 1960, at the time when the Administration secretly committed itself to overthrowing the insolent regime: Castro would be removed "through disenchantment and disaffection based on economic dissatisfaction and hardship [so] every possible means should be undertaken promptly to weaken the economic life of Cuba [in order to] bring about hunger, desperation and [the] overthrow of the government."

Along with his terrorist war, Kennedy imposed a trade embargo of unprecedented severity, barring any transaction involving merchandise "of Cuban origin" or that "has been located or transported from or through Cuba [or] is made or derived in whole or in part of any article which is the growth, produce, or manufacture of Cuba." In the years that followed, huge resources have been devoted to monitor international commerce to ensure that the strictures are upheld—no slight task when it is necessary to ban any product that might include Cuban nickel (Presidents Johnson and Reagan) or Swiss chocolate using Cuban sugar (President Clinton). Allies might be pardoned for regarding "demented" as something of an understatement for these fervent efforts, across the political spectrum.

One illustration has been provided by the Treasury Department, reporting to Congress in April 2004 on the activities of its Office of Foreign Assets Control (OFAC), responsible for investigating suspicious financial transfers, a central component of the "war on terror." OFAC informed Congress that of its 120 employees, four were assigned to tracking the finances of Osama bin Laden and Saddam Hussein, while almost two dozen were occupied with enforcing the embargo against Cuba. From 1990 to 2003, OFAC reported 93 terrorism-related investigations with $9,000 in fines; and 11,000 Cuba-related investigations with $8 million in fines. Nothing changed, apparently, after radical Islamists who had been supported by the CIA came very close to destroying the World Trade Center in 1993, along with far more ambitious plans, barely thwarted. These revelations passed with no report in the press, though there was mention of Senator Max Baucus's condemnation of "the administration's absurd and increasingly bizarre obsession with Cuba" and "misuse of taxpayer money" to punish Cuba, "a dangerous diversion from reality...when the United States faces very real terrorist threats in the Middle East and elsewhere." A "bizarre obsession" that traces back to the early months after the overthrow of the US-backed Batista dictatorship, and reached true fanaticism under Kennedy.

The effort to sustain the righteous punishment of the people of Cuba persists in the face of virtually unanimous global opposition, as demonstrated by the annual votes on the US embargo at the United Nations, where Washington can muster only dependent clients: Israel and some Pacific island. Dismissal of world opinion is of course standard. Also standard is the disregard for public opinion within the US, which for decades has favored normalization of relations with Cuba, by large majorities. More unusual is the fact that the frenzied assault persists in opposition to the will of major concentrations of private power: agribusiness, the pharmaceutical industry, energy corporations, and others. The state interest in crushing Cuba overwhelms even this normally decisive factor in shaping foreign relations.

The "bizarre obsession" appears irrational in the light of any threat posed by Cuba, apart from the quite serious threat in October 1962 that was largely a consequence of the terrorist war—which was designed to culminate that month with "open revolt and overthrow of the Communist regime" that could achieve its "final success" only with "decisive U.S. military intervention." Historian Thomas Paterson concludes, quite plausibly, that "had there been no exile expedition at the Bay of Pigs, no destructive covert activities, no assassination plots, no military maneuvers and plans, and no economic and diplomatic steps to harass, isolate, and destroy the Castro government in Havana, there would not have been a Cuban missile crisis. The origins of the

October 1962 crisis derived largely from the concerted U.S. campaign to quash the Cuban revolution." But apart from self-induced threats, the "hysteria" does appear to pass beyond the bounds of reason.

Irrationality, however, does not entail that there is no rationale, and there most definitely was. Apart from its deep historical roots, the rationale derives rationally from the exigencies of world control. The CIA informed the White House that overthrow of the Castro regime "was the key to all of Latin America; if Cuba succeeds, we can expect most of Latin America to fall." And if we cannot control our own backyard in Latin America, Nixon's National Security Council added, we will not be able "to achieve a successful order elsewhere in the world": that is, to impose our rule over the world. As Henry Kissinger explained while expressing his support for Reagan's terrorist wars in Central America, "if we cannot manage Central America, it will be impossible to convince threatened nations in the Persian Gulf and in other places that we know how to manage the global equilibrium"; to translate into English, we will not be able to rule the world effectively— always for the good of mankind, by definition. Other parts of the world had an even more cosmic significance, particularly the Middle East energy producing regions. Controlling them will provide "substantial control of the world," in the words of the influential planner A.A. Berle, a prominent figure in the Roosevelt and later liberal administrations.

The basic logic was "the domino theory," which has two variants. For the public, the threat is military conquest, as when Reagan strapped on his cowboy boots and declared a National Emergency because Sandinista hordes are only two days from Harlingen Texas, about to overwhelm us, and invaded the nutmeg capital of the world because it might provide a military base for the Russians (if they could find it on a map); and other similar effusions over the years. That version is dismissed with ridicule after it is exposed as absurdity, but the more serious version of the domino theory is never abandoned, because it is entirely reasonable. We might call it "the Mafia doctrine," one of the few pervasive principles of imperial domination—the dedication to ensure "global equilibrium" or "stability," in the preferred euphemism.

The logic is straightforward, and completely rational. The Godfather does not tolerate disobedience. If some small storekeeper fails to pay protection money, the Godfather sends his goons, not just to collect the money, which he wouldn't even notice, but to beat him to a pulp, so that others do not get the idea that disobedience is permissible. He has to ensure that "the virus" does not "spread contagion" elsewhere, to borrow Kissinger's terms when he was dealing with the urgent need to overthrow the parliamentary regime in Chile and impose a regime of killers and torturers—who quickly acted to spread a more acceptable form of "contagion," establishing a brutally efficient international terror center with US backing, Operation Condor.

The Mafia logic regularly applies in international relations. Cuba is an example, but only one of many. In the case of Cuba, the basic problem was clearly perceived at once by the Eisenhower administration. The State Department understood that Castro "rejects the concept that hemisphere defense under U.S. leadership is necessary"— the term "defense" having its usual meaning: control and where necessary aggression. What is more, State warned, Castro "favors a greater role for Latin America, if possible under Cuba's leadership, in world affairs,...as an independent force, associated closely with the Afro-Asian bloc." The latter concerns elicited more hysteria 15 years later when the Portuguese empire fell and Cuba played a leading role— and as historian Piero Gleijeses has demonstrated, a remarkably selfless one—in the liberation of Black Africa and in laying the foundations for the collapse of the US-backed Apartheid regime in South Africa. Eisenhower's State Department warned further that the success of Castro's economic programs might endanger US economic interests in Latin America, perhaps even beyond. Acting Secretary of State Douglas Dillon warned that "If Cuba gets away with the actions she is taking against American property owners [who pretty much owned Cuba], our whole private enterprise approach abroad would be in serious danger."

A basic problem, US Ambassador to Cuba Philip Bonsal explained, is that "Castro continues to enjoy the support of the masses," leading State Department Latin American analyst Calvin Hill to lament the "marked emotional reluctance among many Cubans to face up to the fact that their union with Castro is turning out badly."

The childlike emotionalism of the Latin temperament has always troubled sober and reasonable American officials, again in November 2009, when President Obama broke with Europe and Latin America by supporting the elections carried out under military rule in Honduras, and the US representative to the OAS had to instruct the backward Latin American peons that they should join the US in the real world, abandoning their "world of magical realism," and should recognize the military coup as Big Brother did.

When Kennedy took over from Eisenhower, the CIA spelled out much the same concerns. In July 1961 the CIA observed that "The extensive influence of 'Castroism' is not a function of Cuban power... Castro's shadow looms large because social and economic conditions throughout Latin America invite opposition to ruling authority and encourage agitation for radical change," for which Castro's Cuba provides a model. The same conclusion had already been presented to incoming President Kennedy by Arthur Schlesinger, transmitting the report of his Latin American Mission, which warned of the susceptibility of Latin Americans to "the Castro idea of taking matters into one's own hands." The dangers of the "Castro idea" are particularly grave, Schlesinger later elaborated, when "The distribution of land and other forms of national wealth greatly favors the propertied classes...[and] The poor and underprivileged, stimulated by the example of the Cuban revolution, are now demanding opportunities for a decent living." The Soviet threat was not entirely ignored. Kennedy feared that Russian aid might make Cuba a "showcase" for development, giving the Soviets the upper hand throughout Latin America.

The State Department Policy Planning Council soon expanded on these concerns: "the primary danger we face in Castro," it concluded, is "in the impact the very existence of his regime has upon the leftist movement in many Latin American countries... The simple fact is that Castro represents a successful defiance of the US, a negation of our whole hemispheric policy of almost a century and a half"—that is, back to the Monroe Doctrine, which asserted Washington's intention and right to dominate the hemisphere.

As the charge against Castro indicates, the 50-year crusade to overthrow the Cuban government has deep historical roots. The great grand strategist John Quincy Adams, the intellectual author of the Monroe Doctrine, wrote that "the annexation of Cuba to our federal republic will be indispensable to the continuance and integrity of the Union itself." Thomas Jefferson agreed. He wrote that Cuba's "addition to our confederacy is exactly what is wanted to round our power as a nation... The control which, with Florida Point, this island would give us over the Gulf of Mexico, and the countries and isthmus bordering on it, as well as all those whose waters flow into it, would fill up the measure of our political well-being." His successors found these constraints to be far too modest. The eminent historian John Lewis Gaddis traces "the roots of the Bush doctrine" of preemptive war to the famous state paper of his hero, John Quincy Adams, justifying the murderous invasion of Florida in 1818, also setting the precedent for executive war in violation of the Constitution. Gaddis explains that Adams established the principle that expansion is the path to security, a principle which, he observes sympathetically, has guided political leaders ever since, by now reaching to plans for "ownership of space" for military purposes.

Adams understood that the indispensable conquest of Cuba would have to wait. The British were a powerful deterrent, just as they blocked repeated efforts to conquer Canada. But Adams wisely observed that as US power increased, and Britain's declined, the deterrent would vanish and Cuba would fall into Washington's hands by "the laws of political gravitation," as an apple falls from a tree. By 1898 the laws of political gravitation had worked their magic, and the US was able to carry out the military operation known as "the liberation of Cuba," in reality the intervention to prevent Cuba from liberating itself from Spanish rule, converting it to what historians Ernest May and Philip Zelikow rightly call a "virtual colony" of the US. The Eastern end, including Cuba's major port on Guantánamo Bay, has remained an actual colony, held under a 1902 treaty that Cuba was forced to sign at gunpoint, and used in recent years in violation of the terms of the "treaty," such as it is, as a detention camp for Haitians fleeing the terror of the US-backed military junta and as a torture chamber for those suspected of having harmed, or intended to harm, the US.

The "virtual colony" gained authentic liberation in 1959, apart from its Eastern region. And within months the assault began, using the weapons of violence and economic strangulation to punish the inhabitants of "that infernal little Republic" who had so angered the racist expansionist Theodore Roosevelt "that I would like to wipe its people off the face of the earth," he declared in fury as they continued to rebel, not recognizing that we had set them free. And to this day refusing to comprehend that their role is to serve the master, not to play at independence.

The valuable study that follows permits us to hear the voices of the victims of the international terrorism launched by the Kennedy brothers—for the first time, a remarkable comment on the reigning culture of imperialism in the US and its Western allies.

Noam Chomsky
December 25, 2009

1
The Unknown War

For half a century the Cuban people have endured almost every conceivable form of terrorism. The bombs that have destroyed department stores, hotel lobbies, theaters, famous restaurants and bars—people's lives. The second worst act of air terrorism in the Americas, resulting in the deaths of 73 civilians. An exploding ship in Havana Harbor, killing and injuring hundreds. Attacks on defenseless villages. Teenagers tortured and murdered for teaching farmers to read and write. Biological terrorism causing the deaths of more than 100 children. The psychological horror that drove thousands of parents to willingly send their children to an unknown fate in a foreign country.

Since the earliest days of the revolution, Cuba has been fighting its own war on terrorism. The victims have been overwhelmingly innocent civilians. The accused have been primarily Cuban-American counter-revolutionaries—many allegedly trained, financed and supported by various American government agencies. The justification for this aggression has been framed in the language of ideology, the battle between capitalism and socialism, good and evil. The acts have been described as "disrupting vital resources," "targeting strategic interests," "propaganda efforts." The implication is that military or political objectives have been hit. In reality the majority of the targets have been neither military nor political.

Cuba's war on terrorism has been largely unrecognized by the international community in spite of the material destruction and loss of human life. The government has documented approximately 800 terrorist acts inside Cuba since 1960—hundreds more have occurred against officials and commercial operations outside the country. Each assault has personally affected dozens, if not hundreds; some acts have touched the whole island nation of 11 million. It is hard not to find someone who doesn't have a story to tell of a relative or friend who has been a victim of terrorism. The personal toll has been calculated at 3,478 dead and 2,099 injured.

There are many reasons why few outside Cuba have not heard about this deadly conflict. Cuba is considered to be "the other side." They have a social-political system diametrically opposite to western capitalism. Cuba represents the official enemy. And when it is the United States of America that applies that designation, there is little likelihood this history will be recognized within government elite circles or examined in the mainstream media.

The other reason may be more revealing. Those accused in the vast majority of the acts have been members of anti-Castro militant organizations originating from south Florida. Alpha 66, Omega 7, Commandos F4, are but a few of the more infamous Cuban-American groups that have devoted themselves to the violent overthrow of the Castro regime. The rationalization for these attacks is to bring freedom and democracy to the Cuban people, regardless of the resultant death and destruction. The root cause of the violence is based on the loss of political and economic influence. These groups were organized in the months immediately following the revolution's triumph in January 1959, when the elite of the American-supported Batista dictatorship fled Cuba for the safe confines of Miami, bringing with them organizational skills, financial backing and a visceral hatred for Castro.

Politically the first wave of exiles fit snugly within the US position towards the revolution—hostility, resentment and determination to bring Cuba back under its fold, by whatever methods necessary.

While extreme groups such as Alpha 66 often maneuvered on the fringes of the law, other more respected entities have been accused of also being involved in counter-revolutionary activities, such as Brothers to the Rescue and the Cuban American National Foundation (CANF). The Foundation was established in the 1980s with the assistance of President Ronald Reagan, and has since received government funding in the millions of dollars. Both groups have been implicated in this terrorist war through allegations of financial and material assistance to the more militant groups. And in some cases direct involvement, as in the incident of the biological attack on one of Cuba's most historic tobacco farms by a Cuban-American member of the Brothers, who happened to turn out to be a double agent, according to the farm's famous owner.

Most of these organizations have operated with impunity in the Miami area, many individual members are well-known and admired in the community. Two of the most infamous are Orlando Bosch and Luis Posada Carriles, masterminds of the bombing of Cubana Airlines flight 455 which killed 73 passengers in 1976. Both currently live unmolested in Miami.

Posada Carriles was trained in demolition and guerilla warfare by the CIA in the 1960s, and continued to be an agency operative until the late 1970s. He was involved in the Bay of Pigs invasion, fought with the Contras in Nicaragua, and was arrested in Panama in 2000 for his plan to blow up an auditorium where Castro was lecturing in front of hundreds of students. Posada Carriles has at various times talked extensively to the press about his involvement in terrorist activities against Cuba. In a 1998 interview with the *New York Times*,[1] he spoke in detail about the series of 1997 bombings against Cuban hotel and tourist facilities, which he claimed officials at the Cuban American National Foundation were aware of and helped finance. In the interview he outlined how the explosives were obtained through his contacts in El Salvador and Guatemala, and then carried into Cuba by mercenaries hired by his subordinates.

Carriles admitted the most famous of the hotel bombers, Raúl Ernesto Cruz León, was working for him. It was one of the bombs planted by Cruz León that killed Italian Fabio Di Celmo at the Hotel Copacabana. "That Italian was sitting in the wrong place at the wrong time," Carriles commented in the *Times* article.

Carriles represents the physical manifestation of American policy towards Cuba since the revolution, policy that is unlike any other. While the United States has diplomatic relations with communist Vietnam, considers China one of its most important trading partners, and has never unleashed its wrath against such violators of civil and human rights as Egypt or Saudi Arabia, it continues to hold Cuba up for special punishment. The travel restrictions, the economic blockade, the propaganda war and the terrorist acts have persisted against this small island nation. Since the earliest days of Fidel's victory, America has obsessed over this relatively insignificant third-world country, determined to eliminate the radically different social-economic order instituted by the revolution.

The historical context that has led America to unleash its military, economic and political fury, to allow the launching of thousands of terrorist attacks from its own soil, can be traced back well before Fidel came on the scene. For almost 200 years the United States has looked upon Cuba as part of its natural sphere of influence and has unrelentingly pursued policies to secure that perception. Political and media elites presented this point of view and molded it into historically accepted fact, which became ingrained in the national consciousness. The result is that American dialogue towards Cuba remains consistently confined to narrowly held beliefs.

The certainty that has been most profoundly embedded into the American psyche is over right of possession. The United States convinced itself that ownership of Cuba was natural, preordained, and key to fulfilling vital national expectations. Justifying possession of another country required a sophisticated propaganda campaign. America at various times has portrayed Cuba as a helpless woman, a defenseless baby, a child in need of direction, an incompetent freedom fighter, an ignorant farmer, an ignoble ingrate, an ill-bred revolutionary, a viral communist. These characterizations were designed to demonstrate Cuban inability to control their own country, that to allow them to set up a national government would be misguided at best, dangerous at worst. Only the United States could manage the Cuban population in the proper administration of government, economy and culture. And if any of the locals had the temerity to challenge America's right of possession, they did so at their own peril. In the modern context, the terrorist war against Cuba has as one of its objectives the destruction of the current regime in order to demonstrate incompetence in self-government; thus facilitating reintegration of American interests on the island.

The idea of custody over Cuba goes as far back as 1832 when Secretary of State John Quincy Adams wrote: "There are laws of political as well as of physical gravitation; and if an apple, severed by the tempest from its native tree, cannot choose but fall to the ground, Cuba, forcibly disjoined from its own unnatural connection with Spain, and incapable of self-support, can gravitate only towards the North American Union."[2]

Rationalizations for America's inevitable wresting the island away from Spanish hands came in abundance. The reasoning ranged from proximity to national security.

California Representative Milton Latham conflated both: "Due to its proximity to our shores Cuba is of vast importance to the peace and security of this country." He warned of allowing Cuba to pass to any other hands other than American. "This, not from a feeling of ambitions, not from a desire for the extension of dominion, but because that island is indispensable to the safety of the United States."[3]

Writer William Mills in 1898 bluntly articulated that "The independence of Cuba is, therefore, an historical absurdity... Nothing but her complete incorporation into our territorial system will allay the menace of her geographical position."[4]

With politicians framing the parameters of discussion, and the media in full support, it was an easy matter for the national dialogue to be structured towards the inevitability that America would, and should, own Cuba.

The most opportune chance to control the island presented itself during the last stages of Cuba's Second War of Independence in 1896, known in North America as the Spanish-American war. After three years of fighting between the Cuban rebels and their Spanish overlords, America entered the fray on the noble quest of bringing "freedom" to the Cuban people. At this point both warring sides were at the end of their efforts and the Spanish were indicating a desire to finally cede real independence to the Cuban people. As Fidel Castro said, lecturing to the United Nations General Assembly in September 1960, "Spain had neither the men nor money left to continue the war in Cuba. Spain was routed." Cuba, he noted, was on the verge of true sovereignty for the first time in its history.

America saw the Cuban struggle for independence differently—as the best chance to fulfill its own ambitions. After an intensive public relations drive to convince the public of the necessity of entry into the war, helped by the explosion of the battleship *Maine* in Havana Harbor, United States forces were sent to Cuba in April 1898. Six weeks later the conflict was over. The Treaty of Paris was signed between the United States and Spain on December 10, 1898. There was no Cuban representative at the signing, on the insistence of the American side. This was the start of the historical dialogue that the Cubans had nothing to do with winning their own independence; that national freedom was solely based on the actions of the United States.

Historian Emily Rosenberg described United States intervention as a chivalrous thing, "to provide protection to a woman or to a country— emblematically feminized—that rival men are violating."[5]

The portrayal of Cuba as a helpless woman had another implication: that the Cuban men were ineffective, they could not win their war of independence and so by extension were incapable of running their own country.

The March 15, 1889 edition of the *Philadelphia Manufacturer* described Cuban men as, "Helpless, idle of defective morals, and unfitted by nature and experience for discharging the obligations of citizenship in a great and free republic... Even their attempts at rebellion have been so pitifully ineffective that they have risen little above the dignity of farce."[6]

Editorials such as the one that ran in the *Manufacturer* helped frame the public debate that holding on to the island was the proper thing to do. This despite the expectation of the Cuban side, which believed the Americans would depart gracefully, based on the 1898 Teller Amendment which promised not to annex Cuba but only "leave control of the island to its people." They were in for a rude shock, however, when the United States decided to keep the island for itself.

American control was represented as desirable as it would bring social stability, political maturity and economic prosperity to the child-like Cubans. Naturally then, the Cubans would acquiesce to the wishes of the adult. In this regard local opinion was made irrelevant, as no right thinking person would reject subservience when it brought so much benefit.

Connecticut senator Orville Platt articulated the view, "No man is bound to adopt a child, as we have adopted Cuba; but having adopted a child he is bound to provide for it."[7]

Platt will be forever remembered in the chronicles of modern Cuban–American relations as the man who gave his name to the amendment that best epitomized the policy of wrapping self-interest in the blanket of moral authority. The Platt Amendment was accepted under the strenuous objections of the American-installed Cuban government in 1901. It was finally abrogated in 1934, but by then command was established over all aspects of Cuban social, political and economic life.

The amendment was designed to allow the United States to direct the most important aspects of Cuban society. It was used as a way to ensure that the Cubans would conduct good government with American interests placed first. The other side saw it as an insulting, degrading piece of legislation forced down their throat. It was accepted only when non-compliance would result in the indefinite continuation of the American occupying army. The *New York World* captured the feelings on both sides in its June 14, 1901 editorial cartoon captioned "Down at Last" showing an American military official holding open the baby Cuba's mouth while the politician is force feeding a spoonful of Platt Amendment represented by a large bottle of medicine. In the background the American businessman looks on approvingly from behind a large wooden fence.[8]

Cuba was restricted in a variety of ways under Platt. The amendment gave the Americans control of foreign policy, the right to intervene in

"Down at Last." Depiction of Cuban acceptance of the Platt Amendment. From *New York World*, June 14, 1901.

national affairs, permission for private businesses to come in and invest in Cuba at favorable conditions and the authorization to purchase land at less than market value, with promotions to "colonize Cuba."[9] The Platt Amendment provided the conditions to permit American commerce to dominate the sugar industry and exercise influence over all other aspects of the economy.

The impact of the amendment is still being felt today. Cuba was forced to agree to sell or lease to the United States "lands necessary for coaling or naval stations at certain specified points to be agreed upon." The Americans wanted a large naval base on the south-east end of the island, now known as Guantánamo Bay. Despite Cuba's protests, the treaty allows America to continue to own the Bay until both sides agree to closure.

The most hypocritical condition of the Platt Amendment was the one that prohibited Cuba from negotiating treaties with any country other than the United States, "which will impair or to impair the independence of Cuba" or "permit any foreign power or powers to obtain...lodgement in or control over any portion" of Cuba.

That clause betrayed America's true intentions for Cuba—the United States, a foreign power that was impairing the independence of Cuba, forcing the Cubans to sign a treaty prohibiting them from negotiating treaties to impair their independence. It brought home to the Cubans what Indiana Senator Albert Beveridge snorted in 1900: "Cuba independent. Impossible."[10]

The Cubans chaffed under the Platt Amendment, while the Americans criticized the local population for not showing enough gratitude, nor sufficient appreciation for all that was being bestowed upon them. Within that frame was the precept of never acknowledging the Cuban role in their own struggle for independence—that freedom was only achieved through the spending of American blood and materiel.

"Ungrateful to the last degree for the condescension of the United States in coming to their relief," the *New York Post* complained.[11]

The assumption that this island nation should forever be beholden to American hegemony crashed upon the shores of the revolution. It came as a shock when Fidel Castro started to change the rules of the game, spoken in the determination that no longer would Cuba feel indebted for the dubious historical perspective that America was solely responsible for their liberty. Fidel made it clear that America should no longer naturally assume ownership of Cuba. A new historical reality was being established, far closer to the truth; that the Cubans were the engineers of their own freedom, fought the Spanish heroically, deserved the fruits of independence including self-government of which they were capable of—and that the Americans came in and under the guise of benevolent assistance delayed true Cuban independence for 50 years. That what the Americans brought in the intervening years was the economic advancement of their interests supported and benefited by the acquiescence of a small and compliant Cuban urban elite. American over-lordship did nothing to address the inequalities and suffering of the vast majority of Cubans. The 1959 Revolution was successful because it largely redressed those wrongs that had been fermenting in the Cuban national consciousness since 1898. This was a home grown revolution based on a Cuban national identity of self-worth and pride of accomplishment.

The impetus for revolutionary change in Cuba came under Fulgencio Batista's brutal regime. Batista, who had a leading role in Cuban politics since the 1930s, ran a murderous dictatorship, with American support, from 1952 to the time he left Cuba in late December 1958.

Batista's Cuba in the 1950s was dominated by Havana, the capital city of organized crime in the Americas. Run by the mob, under Batista's co-operative benevolence, Havana was a major drop off point for the narcotics trade in the United States. Drugs, booze, gambling, prostitution, abortions, crime and corruption ran unchecked.

Fidel ended that and promised the revolution would be Cuban, by Cubans, for Cubans. The Americans could not, or would not, understand the new position, seeing their role only as the deliverer of social, economic and political benefits. Fidel shattered that myopia, engendering incredulity that anyone would want to alter, let alone end, those benefits. Incredulity that would eventually manifest itself through policies of hostility, of which terrorism was an important element.

After failing to orient Fidel towards maintaining American primacy, the decision was made to do away with him and his regime. When the revolution was declared to be socialist following the Bay of Pigs invasion in April 1961, the matter to cleanse Cuba of this disease was never further questioned.

Richard Nixon was one of the first to promote the theme of preventing the revolution from infecting others, commented in 1962 on the need to "eradicate this cancer in our own hemisphere."[12]

The politicians and media agreed that whatever steps were needed to rid themselves of this virus were justified, especially when America was sure it did nothing to deserve this ill-treatment from the ungrateful Cubans.

In 1962 American Senator Barry Goldwater reinforced the need for battle based on moral authority and the ingratitude of the Cuban people. "The conditions and attitudes of 1898 have an important and vital bearing on present-day conditions and actions... We won a great victory and we liberated a people. And it cost us dearly. It cost us thousands of lives and millions of dollars." The American victory of 1898 to liberate the Cuban people gave the United States the moral authority to "Use our military and economic strength in the defense of freedom in Cuba. Such a course of action is the type the world should expect from a nation whose blood and heartaches brought freedom for Cuba in the first place."[13]

Goldwater expressed the American foreign policy paradigm that Cuba's gratitude should be eternal. When it became apparent Fidel wouldn't fit into that mold, and then had the temerity to reject American political and economic hegemony, there was no doubt the Cubans had to be liberated again. Deliverance would be attempted through propaganda, economic embargo, invasion and thousands of acts of terrorism against those America deemed had to be "liberated."

Historian Richard Welch crystallized American anger and motives for revenge against Castro on the continued historically misplaced assumption, "that Cuba owned its independence to the United States, and was properly dependent on the latter for its diplomatic security and economic prosperity." That any Cuban leader who dared to challenge these historical facts, and "who sought to destroy Cuba's historic ties with the United States could not be acting from motives of concern for the Cuban people but must be a power-hungry dictator with regional ambitions." It was inconceivable that the Cubans would want anything else but the continuation of America's dominant presence.[14]

Welch and others helped define the attitudes towards the collapse of its Cuban possession—that America was guided exclusively by good deeds, so that any Cuban who disputed this had to be by definition an ingrate, ignoble and evil. Logically, then, whatever Fidel Castro did in opposition to American policy was wrong, regardless of his intentions and strategy towards his own people. All of the revolution's accomplishments in free education, free medical services, the re-distribution of wealth and agrarian land reforms were disregarded, and continue to be discredited. All actions by Fidel were seen through the prism of being against American interests, and were by definition wrong. The only way to deal with Castro and his revolution was to remove him and the disease. In whatever way possible.

Warnings of the dire consequences came fast. For Castro to control Cuba is "a disgrace and an affront which diminishes the respect with which we are held by the rest of the world in direct relation to the length of time we permit it to go unchallenged," Senator Barry Goldwater said in 1961.[15]

South Carolina representative Mendel Rivers angrily reaffirmed America's perceived historical relationship with Cuba in a tirade against Fidel: "That bearded pipsqueak of the Antilles, who seized American property in a country that was conceived by America, delivered by

America, nurtured by America, educated by America and made a self-governing nation by America." He warned of the coming storm between the two nations: "When ingratitude on the part of a nation reaches the point that it has in Cuba, it is time for American wrath to display itself in no uncertain terms."[16]

The actions of both sides made it easier for that American wrath to be warranted as retribution of the aggrieved. The early months saw the United States refuse to buy Cuban sugar or refine oil purchased from the Soviets. The Cubans instituted land reform, confiscating American land (with offers of compensation that were refused), then turned to the nationalization of American industry. As more property was taken, more economic measures were instituted against Cuba. American aggression ran from the embargo, propaganda, isolation, and the Bay of Pigs military invasion. As the rhetoric increased, terrorist acts were formulated and carried out. In partial response to the terror and other hostilities, the revolution became increasingly radicalized.

From the start, policy makers knew terrorism would put a strain politically and economically on the nascent Cuban government, forcing it to use precious resources to protect itself and its citizens. It was to be part of the overarching strategy of making things so bad that the Cubans might rise up and overthrow their government.[17] Terrorism was the dirty piece of the scheme, along with the economic embargo, international isolation and unrelenting approbation.

American officials estimated millions would be spent to develop internal security systems, and State Department officials expected the Cuban government to increase internal surveillance in an attempt to prevent further acts of terrorism. These systems, which restricted civil rights, became easy targets for critics.

CIA officials admitted early on in the war of terrorism that the goal was not the military defeat of Fidel Castro, but to force the regime into applying increasingly stringent civil restrictions, with the resultant pressures on the Cuban public. This was outlined in a May 1961 agency report stating that the objective was to "plan, implement and sustain a program of covert actions designed to exploit the economic, political and psychological vulnerabilities of the Castro regime. It is neither expected nor argued that the successful execution of this covert program will in itself result in the overthrow of the Castro regime," only to accelerate the "moral and physical disintegration of the Castro government." The CIA acknowledged that in response to the terrorist acts the government would be "Stepping up internal security controls and defense capabilities." It was not projected the acts of terror would directly result in Castro's downfall (although that was a policy aim), but only to promote the sense of vulnerability among the population and compel the government into increasingly radical steps in order to ensure national security.[18]

Former agency Director Richard Helms confirmed American strategy when he testified before the United States Senate in 1978: "We had task forces that were striking at Cuba constantly. We were attempting to blow up power plants. We were attempting to ruin sugar mills. We were attempting to do all kinds of things in this period. This was a matter of American government policy."[19]

American experts were hoping the terrorist war would drive the Cuban government to increasingly restrictive security measures; implicit in this was to prove how incapable the regime leaders were. These terrorist acts would not be publicized, recognized or acknowledged outside of Cuba, so national security policies were portrayed as paranoia, totalitarian and evidence of the repressiveness of Fidel's regime. To this day the unknown war remains that way, usually far from the realm of public discourse within current US–Cuba relations.

For the people who have survived, or who have had friends and relatives killed, the terrorist war is always with them—it is anything but unknown.

The terror began early after the Triumph of the Revolution. President Eisenhower agreed to an October 1959 plan to initiate terrorist attacks, to begin March 1960.

The most famous exploits during the early stages were the assassination attempts against Fidel. Supported by the CIA, they ranged from the serious to ridiculous; including poison milkshakes, exploding cigars, or the attempt to cause death by embarrassment by introducing a chemical agent that would have caused El Comandante's beard to fall off.

The furthest reaching aspect of the government strategy was known as The Cuba Project, developed by the CIA with full support from the Eisenhower administration. The Project co-ordinated all types of covert activities, running the gamut from sabotage, assassination, bombings and biological warfare. The most famous offshoot of The Cuba Project was Operation Mongoose, a program of terrorist attacks conducted in the period immediately following the failed Bay of Pigs invasion, aimed primarily at civilians. During Operation Mongoose the newly installed Kennedy administration wanted to bring "the terrors of the earth" to Cuba, in order for the population to throw off their government, historian and Kennedy confidant Arthur Schlesinger reported in his biography of Robert Kennedy.[20] Those terrors included torturing and murdering students who were teaching farmers to read and write, killing Cuban workers showing commercial films in remote villages, blowing up shoppers at Havana's busiest department stores, kidnapping and torturing Cuban fishermen, bombing sugar cane fields and tobacco plantations, and the innumerable attempts to eliminate the top echelon of the government. When the policy was shut down after the October missile crisis, the terrorist activities of the past 30 years were mostly taken over by Cuban-American exiles.

How has Cuban strategy towards its far more powerful northern neighbor been affected by this war on terror? Other than ineffectual complaints to the United Nations, there have only been two options. The most effective has been the infiltration of the terrorist groups in Florida with counter-intelligence agents (which has been accomplished successfully in the past, but has also led to the imprisonment of five agents currently serving jail time in America. The case of the Cuban

Five has drawn international condemnation for its various irregularities during the trial and the unjustly long sentences). The second option has been the implementation of policies to keep its citizens safe, policies that opponents criticize as violating human rights. A third option (or the American first option in its war on terror), to invade the country where the acts are originating from, could never be contemplated. In the early years Cuban officials faced the problem where they couldn't tell which citizens supported the revolution, and which were inclined to assist the terrorist organizations or to commit terrorist acts. Everyone was treated as a potential threat. The consequence, besides the enormous amount of economic resources diverted to combat this war, resources that could have been much better used elsewhere,[21] is a society that in the majority has accepted certain civil restrictions in order to ensure domestic security. It is the way the Cuban government has tried to identify the terrorists and to keep its citizens protected. It is the way the government has fought its war on terror.

While the focus of this project is on the victims and their stories, the work may also offer some illumination on how these acts of terror changed the psyche of the young revolutionary government, struggling to maintain itself in the face of the destructive actions of its former citizens, directed and financed by the most powerful nation in the world. Traumatized by these acts, this small island nation took drastic steps in the face of constant acts of violence. Those reactions to the terrorists, and the measures taken to protect the Cuban people, continue to influence national government policies to this day, and have greatly shaped how Cuba is perceived by the outside world. It is the price that has been paid by a society under siege for almost 50 years. A siege in part the result of the hundreds of acts of terrorism.

The key element of Cuban policy against terrorism has been the need of unity for the sake of security, manifesting in a demand for social and political conformity. The consequence has been extensive surveillance systems, arrests for political crimes, a low tolerance for organized criticism or public displays of opposition, suppression of dissidents seen to have accepted material or financial aid from the United States, cases of institutionalized pettiness, travel restrictions, a state controlled press and the rejection of a more pluralistic society. The demand for social/political conformity has created a hypersensitivity to external criticism that is consistently perceived as a threat to the legitimacy of the regime—and when it comes from the extreme counter-revolutionary elements in Miami it usually is. The siege has also been used to justify some of the limitations and failures of the revolution and the inability of society to advance as expected. Within context, facing this terrorism and aggression from the world's greatest power has offered little other movement but inward, at all times defensive.

The termination of American hostility, including the absolute guarantee of the end to any further terrorist attacks from counter-revolutionary exile organizations, may offer the Cuban government the chance to breathe, to maneuver without a knife at its throat, as Fidel Castro once remarked, and to attempt to develop the Cuban society that was hoped for.[22]

"Today we cannot speak of the pure, ideal, perfect socialism of which we dream because life forces us into concessions. ...oblige us to do what we would never have done otherwise if we had the capital and the technology to do so."[23]

Until then Cuba will remain the modern day embodiment of St. Ignatius Loyola's perception: "In a besieged castle all dissent is treason."

One of the most effective weapons in the terrorist's arsenal is the frightening sense of randomness. The inability of knowing where the next bomb might go off, who else may be tortured and killed, instills fear in the entire population. It is an irrational fear based on actual events. These acts are designed to inculcate the nervous anticipation that the next assault could take place anywhere, anytime, against anyone. It is the sense that these attacks are being aimed against the average person that is terrorism's most effective weapon. The unpredictability leads the population to demand security from their government, and the government to offer it in increasing doses. While the sense of fear is the achievement, the greatest injustice remains the anonymity of the victim. Perversely, the terrorist frequently gains celebrity while those whom he has killed are almost always forgotten. The whole world knows Osama Bin Laden; how many can name a dozen of his victims?

Everyone in Cuba is aware of the heinous act that brought down Cubana Airlines flight 455 in 1976, killing all 73 on board. Assuredly, the vast majority know of the two masterminds of the bombing, Luis Posada Carriles and Orlando Bosch. The pair are also well recognized in Miami, and are treated by the majority of the extreme right Cuban-American community from the opposite perspective—not as terrorists but freedom-fighting heroes.

Far fewer remember the names of the Cuban national fencing team that were on board. Or the small contingent of fishermen coming home after finishing a successful contract in Guyana. Or the family members of the crew, the stewardesses, the others who lost their lives on that flight.

Until now the victims and their families of Cuba's long war on terrorism have never had the chance to tell their stories. They have remained unheard, unknown. Until now.

The array of terrorist acts that has been committed against Cuban citizens is impressive as it is insidious, including 14 young men and women murdered solely for teaching farmers to read and write, while others were killed for showing Hollywood films to the rural population. Hundreds were blown to pieces when the munitions ship *La Coubre* exploded in Havana harbor, a deliberate act of sabotage. Dozens of sugar cane fields have been fire bombed; in the early 1970s almost half a million pigs had to be destroyed after an intentionally introduced swine fever epidemic obliterated Cuba's main food staple. It was the first ever outbreak of the disease in the Western hemisphere. According to Warren Hinckle and William Turner, co-authors of *The Fish is Red*, a US intelligence officer passed a vial of the virus to a terrorist group, who smuggled it into Cuba.[24] At the time the United Nations Food and Agricultural Organization unsuccessfully tried to determine how the disease was transmitted. The only conclusion was that it was introduced from outside the country. Biological terrorism continues to this day in the form of tobacco fungus and eye conjunctivitis; diseases unknown to Cuba until introduced by counter-revolutionaries as a way to terrorize the population and disrupt the economy, authorities claim. The Cuban government maintains a yearly program to control hemorrhagic Dengue 2, conveyed in the early 1980s by a Cuban-American pilot from Florida, according to the testimony of Eduardo Arocena, who confessed in 1984 to introducing certain germs into Cuba to start a chemical war.[25] Arocena was connected to Omega 7, one of the dozens of anti-revolutionary groups based in Miami. Hundreds died from Dengue 2, mostly children, before the disease was identified. The government continues to spend hundreds of thousands of dollars in an annual spraying program.

One of the most sinister forms of terrorism occurred in the early 1960s during what became known as Operation Peter Pan, when religious and government officials in Miami, supported by the Catholic Church in Cuba, convinced thousands of parents to abandon their children and send them out of the country. Before the lies of this psych-op program were exposed, an estimated 14,000 children were dispatched to Florida, many to abusive foster homes, orphanages or church houses where they experienced various levels of mistreatment. In a great number of cases families were never reunited.

Neither the weak nor the young have been spared—120 children, 55 women and 35 seniors have lost their lives during these terrorist attacks.

This book is an effort to create an oral history from a small portion of the thousands of Cuban citizens, young and old, who have been affected by these acts of terror. Additionally, it serves to re-enforce the truth that innocents are not judged by what economic or political system they live under. Freedom fighters that kill teachers, farmers and children are not fighting for freedom, only anarchy. And that terrorism is just as devastating on a personal level to those who are considered to be on the other side.

The anguish felt by Ana Elba Caminero at having lost one daughter to Dengue 2 while seeing another struggle for survival is just as real and powerful as any mother's despair. The scars remain as deep. The anger of finding out that this deadly disease was introduced intentionally is just as intense. And the sorrow of losing a child is just as heart rending.

Others who have lived in silence with their pain and suffering now have the chance to tell their stories:

Nancy Pavón struggling for her life as a 15-year-old girl after having her foot shot off during the attack on the village of Boca de Samá. Nancy and her family endured a night of terror before finally escaping with their lives.

Felipe Quintero Diaz replaced at the last minute on the same Cubana Airlines flight by his best friend Manuel Permuy. Felipe stayed, and has lived with the guilt ever since.

Juan Luis, who lost his leg in the explosion of *La Coubre* munitions ship in Havana Harbor while helping to save others, including Fidel Castro and Ché Guevara, from a burning truck full of grenades.

Maria Dolores Ascunce, sister of Manuel, one of the more than a dozen students who were tortured and killed for teaching adults to read and write during the Literacy Campaign of the early 1960s.

This book is an attempt to put a human face on those who live in a country that is a jumble of contradictions, most often portrayed in negative terms. Those interviewed share a common bond as victims of this long war on terrorism. Individually, their human qualities are distinct and are on display all the more intensely; imperfections and all.

The written style is *testimonio*—a common Latin Americana genre taking a memory of a particular event. It is seldom a remembrance of a whole life, and is told specifically from the individual's point of view with all its limitations and failings—with the emotions and immediacy still in place. The intent is also to make sure the past is not forgotten.

Of all the terrorist acts committed against Cuba, none has been more shattering than the bombing of the Cubana Airlines airplane in 1976. It remains the second most destructive act of air terrorism in North America, after 9/11.

2

Cubana Airlines

On October 6, 1976 Cubana Airlines flight 455 flew from Guyana to Trinidad/Tobago on a journey that was to continue on to Barbados, with a scheduled stop in Jamaica before its final destination Havana.

This was the regularly scheduled itinerary Cubana de Aviación had been operating under for more than ten years. The flight was a little out of the ordinary as it was carrying a special group of passengers—the Cuban national fencing team coming home from its victory at the Central American championships in Caracas. The team, which had flown from Venezuela to Trinidad in order to connect with the Cubana flight, dominated the competition, winning all 22 gold medals. Made up mostly of athletes in their early 20s, they were in a festive mood and the enthusiasm was contagious among the other travellers, consisting of various sports officials as well as a small group of Cuban fishermen and five North Koreans. In total there were 48 passengers and 25 crew.

Cubana Airlines flight 455 was special for another, quite different reason.

The DC-8 arrived at Seawell International Airport in Barbados at 11:21 a.m., scheduled to depart for Jamaica an hour later. Everyone, with the exception of two Venezuelan nationals, remained on the plane. Freddy Lugo and Hernan Ricardo had boarded the plane in Port of Spain with the intention of planting two bombs in the rear part of the aircraft a few minutes before landing in Barbados. The plastic C-4 explosives, concealed in a photographer's bag, were timed to go off approximately one hour after takeoff, giving the two men ample time to disembark and return to Trinidad.

Due to labor problems at the airport, the Cubana takeoff was delayed until 12:45 p.m. Flight 455 was in the air for approximately nine minutes when the first bomb, placed in seat 10 beside the left wing, went off. The second was in the rear washroom, the detonation tearing out the steering controls of the plane, forcing it for a few moments into a steep ascent. After the first blast the crew desperately tried to get the plane back to the airport, turning the craft around and reaching to within three miles of the coast before the second bomb went off, splitting the plane in two. From the time of the first explosion to the plane crashing into the sea less than five minutes had passed.

The recording recovered later revealed the last terrifying moments. In a voice since heard thousands of times in Cuba, co-pilot Miguel Espinosa Cabrera screamed to pilot Wilfredo Pérez Pérez during the forced ascent ... "That's worse. Head toward the water. Felo, head toward the water."

Moments later fishermen off the Barbados shore reported seeing this mass, now more a fireball than an aircraft, crash into the water. In a few hours those same fishermen were picking up the hundreds of objects that had washed ashore from the wreckage. Only eight bodies were ever recovered.

The two Venezuelans had miscalculated the timing of the bombs. Lugo and Ricardo were still in the airport vicinity when the plane went down and later testified to their astonishment when the DC-8 exploded so soon after takeoff. The plan was to have it destroyed over open waters, where any evidence would be impossible to recover. The pair had failed to take into account the delay caused by the striking airport staff.

Shortly after the aircraft exploded the authorities were checking over the master passenger list. It was not difficult to determine there were two passengers who boarded the plane in Trinidad without check-in luggage, then disembarked in Barbados. Lugo and Ricardo were arrested back in Port of Spain a day later.

Cuban officials received word of the explosion on the afternoon of October 6, although the cause was yet to be confirmed. Then Cuban ambassador to the United Nations, Ricardo Alarcón was scheduled to speak at the General Assembly and once informed he called for an immediate investigation.

Ricardo Alarcón

Since 1992 Alarcón has been President of Cuba's National Assembly, one of the most powerful positions in the country. He remembers vividly the action taken over the following days following the downing of the Cubana Airlines plane.

"The two material witnesses [Lugo and Ricardo] were captured in Puerto Spain, Trinidad. In the meantime by coincidence two leaders of the countries involved were also in New York to address the General Assembly—Venezuelan President Carlo Andrés Pérez, and Tom Adams the newly elected Prime Minister of Barbados. I spoke to Tom before I spoke at the General Assembly."

The expressive Alarcón, who served for years as Cuba's Minister of Foreign Affairs, arranged with Barbados officials for the return of any of the remains. The Cuban government was preparing a memorial at the Plaza de la Revolución in Havana, an event which attracted more than 1 million mourners.

Alarcón then headed to Barbados where he met with Cuban and Barbadian officials. Two parallel inquiries were organized; one criminal investigation in Trinidad and the other the technical examination of the incident in Barbados. The Barbados study concluded that the crash was the result of two explosions in the cabin area, not in the luggage compartment. This showed that the bombs were brought on in person, and that those responsible either committed suicide, or left the plane after planting the explosives.

"Trinidad, for their part, took into custody the two suspects and they talked about who planned it," Alarcón remembered.

During the interrogations both Lugo and Ricardo confessed that Luis Posada Carriles and Orlando Bosch were the masterminds behind the plot. It was soon determined that Ricardo was employed by Posada at his private detective agency based in Venezuela, where the plot was hatched. At the time of the bombing Posada was a Venezuelan citizen, working with the country's secret police. Ricardo had recruited his friend Lugo to join him in the plan.

Posada and Bosch, rabid anti-Castro activists, have been accused of various act of terrorism going back to the early 1960s. Bosch, a Cuban-American, was arrested in Florida in 1968 for an attack on a Polish freighter in Miami harbor. The freighter was on its way to Cuba. He has been linked to more than 50 bombings against Cuban civilian targets.

Posada was a member of the Cuban-American brigade that invaded Cuba at the Bay of Pigs in 1961. A CIA agent in the 1960s and 70s, he was accused of actions against Cuban officials outside the country, and during the 1980s was involved with the Contras in Nicaragua. He was also implicated in the bombings of Cuban hotels in 1997, resulting in the death of Italian tourist Fabio Di Celmo.[1] Posada was arrested in 2000 during an attempt to assassinate Fidel Castro at a conference at the University of Panama where he was scheduled to speak. Authorities discovered more than 33 pounds of C-4 plastic explosives in the auditorium, which would have killed hundreds of Panamanian students along with Castro. In 2004 Posada was sentenced to prison for his part, but four months later then Panamanian President Mireya Moscoso issued a pardon. Moscoso, who left office soon after, now lives in Miami. The pardon has subsequently been called unconstitutional and demands have been made for the return of Posada.[2]

Following Lugo's and Ricardo's testimony, Posada and Bosch were arrested in Venezuela. Shortly after it was decided all four would be tried there.

Before the trial began, Venezuelan President Carlos Andrés Pérez made a public appeal to the United States government asking for co-operation with the investigation.

As Alarcón stated, the Venezuelan president wanted to clear up "The rumors and speculation in the media, everyone was talking about the CIA's involvement in the bombing. The president of Venezuela said that for the sake of US prestige it was important for them to dispel all these speculations and assist in the efforts to get to the truth. As it turned out, the CIA did know about this."

Government documents released in 2005 showed United States officials were aware in advance of the possibility of the downing of a Cubana Airlines flight, and that Bosch and Posada were implicated. There is no evidence of American government involvement in the bombing, although hundreds of documents relating to the bombing continue to be restricted.

In 2008 the National Security Archive released three declassified FBI intelligence reports that were sent to Secretary of State Henry Kissinger after the bombing. The updates, classified "secret" and signed by director Clarence Kelly, focused on the relations between the FBI legal attaché in Caracas, Joseph Leo, Posada, and one of the Venezuelans who placed the bomb on the plane. One report from Kelly, based on the word of an informant in Venezuela, suggested that Posada had attended meetings in Caracas where the Cubana bombing was planned.

The document also quoted an informant as stating that after the plane went into the ocean Hernan Ricardo placed a frantic call from his hotel room in Barbados to Posada and stated: "A bus with 73 dogs went off a cliff and all got killed." He then called a Senior Paniagua, the code name at that time for Bosch. A few hours after the calls Ricardo and Lugo flew back to Trinidad. A declassified CIA document dated October 12, 1976, quotes Posada as saying at a meeting for CORU (Coordination of United Revolutionary Organizations) a month before the bombing, "We are going to hit a Cuban airliner... Orlando has the details."[3]

The FBI has described CORU, co-founded by Bosch, as "an anti-Castro terrorist umbrella organization." CORU members have been accused of taking part in a variety of terrorist activities against Cuba, as well as organizing the assassination in 1976 of Chilean former minister Orlando Letelier, in Washington DC. Just days after the Cubana Airlines bombing CORU released a statement claiming responsibility for the bombing, stating Flight 455 was a military plane disguised as a civilian aircraft.[4]

Almost a year after the bombing the Venezuelan government directed Judge Delia Estévez Moreno to refer the case to a military tribunal. Posada, Bosch and the two bombers were charged with treason. Three years later, in 1980, all were acquitted by a military judge. Immediately after the verdict the prosecutor appealed, arguing convincingly that a military court was the wrong forum as none of the four belonged to the military. The Military Court of Appeals agreed and turned over jurisdiction to the civilian side.

The four were then charged with aggravated homicide and treason before a civilian court. It took almost another five years, until August 1985, before Venezuelan judge Alberto Pérez Marcano of the 11th Penal Court sentenced Lugo and Ricardo to 20 years in prison. The two served their sentences and were released. Lugo is currently driving a taxi in Venezuela. Ricardo's whereabouts are less certain; some say he is dead, others claim he is living in Miami.

While Lugo and Ricardo received long sentences, Orlando Bosch was acquitted due to a technicality, as the evidence gathered in Barbados was not received in time and not translated into Spanish. Bosch was released from Venezuelan charges in 1987, shortly after returning to the United States illegally. Upon entering the United States he was detained by immigration authorities for violating parole on his charges over the attack on the Polish freighter. The Justice Department declared Bosch one of the Western hemisphere's most deadly terrorists, determined he was a threat to public security and requested his deportation.[5] However, those wishes were overridden by President Bush Sr. who issued Bosch a full pardon in 1990. The pardon was made at the request of Bush's son Jeb, who was then campaign manager for Ileana Ros-Lehtinen, a staunch anti-Castroite running for Congress in Miami. Jeb Bush later became Governor of Florida.

The final accused, Posada, had been found not guilty by the military court, but this judgment was overturned and he was held for trial in a civilian court. He was imprisoned for eight years before escaping from the San Juan de los Morros penitentiary on the eve of the pronouncement of his sentence. He had been confined in this prison following two previous failed escape attempts. Allegations were made that Venezuelan authorities were bribed to help him escape. No verdict was entered against Posada because, according to the Venezuelan Penal Code, judicial proceedings cannot continue without the presence of the accused. The court issued an arrest warrant against him which is still pending.

Posada returned illegally to the Untied States in 2005 asking for political asylum and like Bosch, was arrested on immigration violations. He was released of those charges in 2007. In 2009 he was then indicted on claims he lied about his involvement in the 1997 bombing campaign against Cuban tourist facilities. A deportation order for the Venezuelan citizen has yet to be resolved, and Cuba has called for Posada to be returned to Venezuela to stand trial, but the United States has refused

Billboard in Havana commemorating the Cubana Airlines bombing.

stating they fear Posada would be tortured. Venezuelan officials have denied those charges. Posada is currently seeking United States citizenship.

Both Bosch and Posada are now living freely in Miami.

Orlando Bosch:

"There were no innocents on that plane."—When referring to the victims of the 1976 Cubana Airlines terrorist bombing.

Luis Posada Carriles:

"The CIA taught us everything, how to use explosives, to kill, to make bombs... they trained us in acts of sabotage."—Interviewed by *NY Times*, July 12, 1998.

The United States has never formally recognized the downing of Cubana Airlines 455 as an act of terrorism.

HAYMEL ESPINOSA GÓMEZ

Haymel Espinosa Gómez is a welcoming, quick speaking woman who has deep, dark eyes. She is the Cubana Airlines bombing unofficial archivist, holding an extensive collection of articles, books and photos, all kept in a series of thick black binders. Haymel has kept the memory of her father alive through this huge personal library. In addition, she is extremely active in the Committee of the Family Victims of the Cubana Airlines Bombing in Barbados.

Haymel Espinosa Gómez
and her mother Eudelia

Haymel's father Miguel was the co-pilot of the aircraft. His voice became one of the most recognizable in Cuba following the recovery of the black box, as it was he who was heard screaming at the pilot to head closer to the ocean.

Her mother, Eudelia, was at first reluctant to participate in the interview. When asked of her recollection of the day, she said nothing for a few moments, her eyes dry but her mouth tight. Finally she spoke, and with some encouragement from her daughter she opened up; offering information about her husband—how they met, their life together and her difficulties after the bombing.

The family has gone through more than their share of hardship. Besides losing the head of the family, Haymel's brother was also a pilot who died in a plane accident. Eudelia has had heart problems for many years, forcing the family to survive on a small government pension. Despite the setbacks, Haymel was able to graduate from medical school and is now an orthopedic surgeon. Throughout the conversation Haymel directs attention to specific pages of her collection, pointing out the rally at Havana's Revolutionary Square held shortly after the bombing. She makes precise mention of Fidel Castro's declaration at the rally in 1976—"When a country cries, injustice trembles."

"More than a million people attended this rally in Revolution Square to hear Fidel's speech two weeks after Barbados. Then, 25 years later on October 6, 2001, the same number attended the Square to mark the anniversary. My function with all this is to ask for justice. In 2001 we sent a message to those victims of September 11, to show that their pain is in solidarity with ours, and to offer sympathy. The suffering is similar, and we've been suffering for more than 30 years. Once a year we'd get together, but after September 11 the emotions we all felt were stronger. So all the families get together more often."

Haymel stops talking, turning the pages on the binder slowly as she looks intensely at the articles and photos. Her conversation turns to those accused of masterminding the bombing.

"The Cuban government could have captured Posada many times, but our country's policy is not to do it that way. Public opinion is very important, the international community must be made aware of this, to know our pain is the same as anyone who has suffered terrorist attacks. There is no difference to what we have gone through to the victims of September 11, or other victims."

Haymel admits it is still hard to come to grips with how her father died.

"If a person passes away from sickness, or old age, that's normal. You can accept that. But when someone is killed and you see the person who killed them hasn't been charged—you will never have the peace in your soul. But at least you can try for justice. Not for revenge, just to let the world know what has happened here, and for those responsible to be held accountable, not treated as heroes. The two who put the bombs on the plane were charged and paid a penalty, but those who arranged the bombing nothing has happened. My father? I don't think he is resting in peace. So I continue this work, it is all I can do, it is a spiritual thing."

Slowly she starts going over the details of the day. "Normally the pilots are home by noon. On that day the calls came—people asking if my dad was home. No one knew anything but everyone knew something. On that day, my mother was supposed to come to my school to help paint it. The people kept calling, saying they had a bad premonition.

"A friend was listening to a radio, one that received signals from outside Cuba, and he heard an announcer say a plane exploded in Barbados, and it was a Cubana Airline. At 8 p.m. the Cuban government made an announcement about the plane, but my mother and I were still out, we weren't at home so we didn't know anything."

Eudelia nods her head in agreement, her eyes fixed on her daughter. She then adds her memories of that day, and how she met her husband.

"In Cuba, you know, all the neighbors know everything before you do. So I felt something was wrong, but I couldn't say anything. I didn't want to worry my daughter. I know she says she knew and didn't want to worry me, but I also knew something and didn't want to worry her. Then someone came to get us and said there was an accident, but they didn't know what happened, if there were any survivors. When we got home our house was filled with people. But still no one knew anything definite. At 11 p.m. that night we were told the plane was bombed, no one left alive.

"My husband, he was a radio worker. He was always very good at fixing electronic things. He was working in a factory, and by mistake one day he called my phone. I answered, and he said it was Miguel. I thought it was someone I knew. But it was this other person, I didn't know him. We talked and talked and we agreed to meet afterwards. One year later we were married.

"He was in the mountains with the revolutionaries before we met. We met in 1960, and the revolution triumphed in 1959, so it wasn't long after that. My family was all from Havana, and when my mother found out we were dating she told me he's just a *guajiro* [the term is a Cuban slang for the English 'war hero'—the Cubans use it as a term for the uneducated farmers who went to fight in the revolution. The origins are from the Spanish-American war. Today it's meant disparagingly for someone who is unsophisticated.] He'd come over to our house with dirty clothes and not good manners. He was a *barbudo* [bearded—a phrase to describe those unshaven ones who fought in the mountains during the revolution] and my mother was not happy. But she didn't say anything, and after we fell in love and got married."

Haymel relates that her father's work ethic instilled the same dedication in her. "I studied very hard to become a doctor and I still love to study. I got that from my father. He was a kind, loving person. I remember he'd always bring me something when he came back from a flight. A candy, a toy, something. It wouldn't matter if I was asleep or not, he'd come home and wake me up and show me what he brought. My mother would always tell us not to complain that my father was away so much, that there would be time in the future that he'd be able to spend a lot of time with us." She falls silent again, her eyes fall to the photos in the binder. A moment later a grin appears.

"This is a funny story," she says. "I just remembered it now. One day my father had something wrong with his foot. I was a kid, but I told him I can fix it. So I got some scissors and by mistake I cut him. He was bleeding, but he laughed and said I'd never be a doctor. Now look, I have become an orthopedic surgeon."

Haymel recalls another incident, not as happy, as to how her father had a premonition of what was to come.

"There was a bomb put on another Cuban DC-8 plane that my father was the pilot of. It was June 1976, flying to Jamaica, just a few months before the Barbados explosion. This one in June, the bomb didn't explode. He could have been killed in that one. I remember later he told my mother he had a feeling he'd be killed one day in a plane.

"When my father talked about these other incidents my mother took it as a joke, I don't think she wanted to think about it. My mother would say to my dad, 'Don't get yourself killed, the only thing left would be they'd put your name on a school or something.' After he died, they didn't put his name on a school, but he is remembered. I was in Barbados a number of years ago, the government there put up a monument to those who lost their life in the bombing. There is a list of all the names of those who were killed, and my father's name is there. I want to take another trip to Barbados, to finish the flight my dad never could. I would ask the pilot to fly right over the spot the plane went down."

While few bodies were recovered afterwards, divers were able to retrieve the aircraft's black box. In it were the recordings of the final few minutes, as crew members understood an explosion had torn the back half of the jet apart. The most recognized part of that recording is Haymel's father screaming: "Eso es peor, pegate al agua Felo, pegate al agua." That's worse, head towards the water, Felo (the pilot's nickname), head towards the water.

After a response from another plane there is silence.

"That's my father's voice in the plane going down. The first time I heard it, it was a torture, it was so bad. But it has been played here so many times in Cuba, millions of times, I can turn it off now when I hear it."

Eudelia adds her thoughts hesitantly, the only time it appears emotion may overcome her.

"They were fighting for their lives, to hear his voice and the others is terrible. I can't imagine what they were going through, trying to save the plane. How the others were reacting. The hardest was when the kids, and the grandchildren would ask, 'Is this my grandpa talking?' I tell them yes, but I don't give them details. It is too hard."

JORGE DE LA NUEZ OROZCO

Jorge De La Nuez Orozco is completely lost within the memory.

"I remember that day, running up to see my mom on the top of the stairs. I was so excited, so happy to think I was going to see my father. Then to see my mother's face, sad, crying, finding out that my father... It is like it happened yesterday." In fact, it's been more than 30 years since Jorge De La Nuez was told he'd never see his father again.

De La Nuez, 38, relates the story of his father's death with a surprising amount of tenderness, despite the raw emotion it still brings out. Like most Cubans, he lives for his family. Jorge smiles readily, laughs constantly and displays an endearing inner strength. He lives in a modest, small second floor apartment in Havana, with his child, wife and mother.

Jorge De La Nuez with his mother Niuvis and son Jorge Jr.

Jorge's mother Niuvis was asked to participate in the interview, but declined. Protesting that the memory is still too difficult to talk about, "It makes me too emotional, my blood pressure will rise." She excuses herself, saying she is going to visit a sick friend, and doesn't want to feel worse by talking about her husband. Later, however, she relents and agrees to be interviewed at a future date. Her memory of the tragedy carries with it the added pain of a dreadful coincidence.

Jorge sits down at his kitchen table and pulls out a few old, red-tinted photos of a group of men sitting around a counter, drinking and having a good time. The photo includes his father, who also carried the name Jorge.

The picture was taken while the group of shrimp fishermen were celebrating in Guyana, in recognition of a record catch of 1,128 kg. Jorge Sr. was head of the delegation and the photo was taken only three days before the group died on the ill-fated Cubana Airlines flight.

He speaks slowly at first, looking at the picture, cautiously moving his fingers over the image of his father.

"In my mind October 6, the day the plane went down, is not important. I didn't know the specific date my dad was coming back. But that day, in my mind, is like it happened yesterday. I was in school, seven years old at the time, and I was behaving badly. I wasn't listening to my teachers, because I was waiting for my father to come home from his trip. My father was my life, more than my mother, he was the one who was more important. I think this is true of most boys. I used to see my life through my father's eyes.

"A friend of my parents came to see me at school that day, to pick me up. I knew him well, and it reminded me that I was going to my dad. When I got into his car he couldn't say anything, he didn't have the strength to tell me anything, because I was so happy that I was going to see my father. All during the drive I kept asking this friend, 'How is my father, is he fat, how is he, did my father bring me anything, did he bring me any toys, or something?' I was so excited. And he only said my mother will explain everything to me. He knew what had happened to the plane. He knew my father was dead.

"So I got home and went upstairs, at the top of the stairs I saw my mother, and she was crying. It was a shock, a hit, to see her crying. I thought 'why would she be crying?' My dad is home and she should be happy. When I got to her she grabbed me and gave me a hug, she hugged me hard. She gave me a kiss. She said 'oh my son' and I replied 'what's the matter mom?' She said once again 'oh my son, something terrible has happened.' And I start screaming 'What, what happened, where is my dad? Why are you crying? You have to be happy.' My mother told me my dad was not coming back. I thought, well he's not coming home today, when is he coming home? But she said that my dad has been in an accident. She said my father would not be coming home, ever."

Jorge pauses for a moment, reliving the day with a half-smile on his face, gathering himself emotionally before continuing.

"I thought, how could my father not come home, he's cheating me. My mother said he had an accident and we can't see him any more. I cried and cried. I didn't understand death, but I was sad that I wouldn't be able to see him ever again. It was such a trauma, such a difficult time. Many days passed that I wasn't eating, that I was crying, that I was refusing everything.

"I couldn't talk about this for such a long time. Little by little I started to understand more of what happened. I heard Fidel speak of it. I thought he was going to say they had got all the people who did this and they were in jail. It was about five years after that before I was able to get over the trauma and to understand that the plane was bombed, that it exploded out of the sky and everyone was killed."

He continues, reluctantly, to relive the effect the accident had on his teenage years and his education.

"I wasn't the same kid any more. I failed my first year of college. I also had some altercations with guys at the school and instead of them saying 'fuck your mom' to insult me; they would say 'fuck your dad,' so I became very violent. My college years were full of problems. I finished my college years in a different school and then after I went to a maritime school. I always had two things that I loved the most—my father and the sea. Nowadays if I have a problem, to clear my mind I go to the sea, because I know my dad is both in the sea and in the air and going there I feel at peace."

His thoughts turn to the final few moments of the Cubana airliner. And the ache he and the other families of the victims go through every October 6, the anniversary of the bombing.

"When I think of the plane, I think of the pain, of the people on board in that moment. I try to imagine what they were thinking, what was happening to them. The total confusion, the panic, then death. Why did that happen, because someone has another point of view? For politics? These were not military men, or top government officials on that plane. These were average people, young, old, with brothers, sisters, wives, husbands, children. It was filled with the athletes of the fencing team, they were celebrating winning the championship in Venezuela. That's who they were."

NIUVIS DE LA NUEZ

Jorge's mother Niuvis was interviewed on October 25, 2007. It is a month that holds both special and dreadful memories for her as she is forever linked to the 10th month of the year. The worst part of that time is the terrible coincidence of having her wedding anniversary on the same date her husband died—October 6.

The interview has taken six months to arrange, and when greeted at the door she's ready, in a fine patterned dress with white kerchief tied tightly around her short black hair. She is still hesitant to talk, but warms rapidly to the topic of her husband, and the remarkable story of how they met.

"There are so many coincidences on this date, this month of October has so much meaning for me. In October, Jorge's parents met. My mother and father were married on October, 12. Jorge and I got married, October 6, the date he died when the Cubana plane went down. It was my second marriage, and my second daughter was born on October 10. There is so much happiness, and sadness, when that month comes. I start thinking of October months before it arrives. What has happened to me, it is for others to say, but for any person who goes through this, it is terrible.

"I am religious, I believe in fate, and when October comes, every year when this month comes, the only thing I think of is that I am going to die. I'm sure when my hour comes I will die in October. Yes, I want it to be October when I die.

"When Jorge and I met we talked about a formal wedding, and he wanted to get married in October, because of all these dates. So that's how our wedding date was decided. It was such a joy, for both families, to have us married in October. We were married October 6, 1961. He died October 6, 1976. I think of him constantly, but that day even more. It is a cruel coincidence.

"The day the plane exploded, Jorge was not originally scheduled to return. His contract with the fishermen in Guyana was not ending until December. My daughter's birthday was October 10, but I told her it wasn't possible to celebrate it then because her dad was still in Guyana working. Well, she got very upset, and so Jorge decided to come back in October, celebrate her birthday, then return to finish the contract. It was going to be a surprise, some people knew, but I didn't. He was just going to walk in the door and surprise everyone. The plane he came back on, it was this plane that exploded. He wasn't even supposed to be on it."

Niuvis pauses, falling silent in her thoughts. Her eyes remain intense and her voice steady as she recalls how Jorge's persistence and determination won her heart.

"I met Jorge in 1960, he belonged to the Cuban navy. I used to work in a hardware store, in Havana. He used to go to an apartment building to visit his work mates. The apartments were above the hardware store where I worked. He'd go inside the store, then go out, then went in again, so many times," she smiles and lets out a soft laugh. "Finally one day he got up his courage and he decided to ask me out. My reaction? I told him not to bother, I'm not interested. At that time I was divorced with two girls. I was living with my mother and I said to myself never again would I marry.

"But Jorge kept asking and asking, and I kept saying don't bother me. So then I made up a story, and I told him if I was ever to marry again I would want to live in my own home. So he said if those are the conditions, OK. Then he left. Honestly, I was relieved; I thought he wasn't going to bother me anymore.

"Then one day, I don't remember how much time passed, maybe a month or so, I was in the back warehouse of the store. One of the other workers said to me, 'the admiral is coming.' I thought what admiral, who is he talking about? Then I saw it was Jorge and I shouted out, 'I'm not here.' But he saw me already and he said, 'If you don't come out to talk to me I won't leave.' So I had no choice, I had to go see him." Niuvis is back to the moment, speaking with her head raised, smiling widely, her voice increasing in tone. "So I came out, and he had this bag. He took out a set of keys from this bag and threw them on the table. I told him we don't make keys here. And he said, I remember this to this day, he said—'It's too bad you are so beautiful but you forget things so easily.' Why, I asked. And he told me, 'That the only way I could marry you is if you had your own home. Well, here are the keys to the home.' I didn't believe it, I stared, saying nothing, he started laughing, then I laughed and the workers all came out and it was something.

"He said, 'I know you don't love me now but I'm sure you'll love me eventually.' He also gave me time to get to know him, very slowly. We didn't move in right away into this house, it took us three or four months to get to know each other before we moved in. It was such a beautiful house."

CARLOS MANUEL PERMUY DIAZ

Carlos Manuel Permuy Diaz sits in a hard wooden chair at his large dining room table. He selects his words carefully, intensely. He's eager to be understood. His outlook on life, and politics, are still being influenced by his father. Carlos lives in a comfortable middle-class home in Havana. Traffic noise combines with the near constant barking of his, and his neighbor's, dogs.

His father, Manuel Permuy Hernandez was head of the delegation of the Cuban fencing team on the Barbados flight. While not a direct member of the fencing team, the father was working for INDER—the Cuban sports federation, and was assigned to the group to co-ordinate the logistics for the competition in Venezuela. Manuel was not originally scheduled to head this sports delegation, but was selected when it was decided he would be better suited to conduct various contractual arrangements with the Venezuelan counterparts. A close friend of Manuel, Felipe Quintero, was the person first picked to head the group, and it was Manuel who took his place on the plane. An interview with Felipe Quintero follows.

Carlos Manuel Permuy Diaz

Carlos Manuel Permuy speaks caringly of his father. "My father was very active athletically, he liked to play basketball, baseball, and he was very much involved in the Cuban national basketball team. He was not a fencer, didn't know the fencing team participants at all, but was assigned to head the delegation.

"Me? Well, in sports, I played a lot, as everyone does in Cuba. But my problem was I didn't have any discipline. My father didn't mind, he just wanted me to be happy. But I felt compromised with him and wanted to make him proud and maybe that's why I ended up working for INDER as well, in the international relations section. As a way to honor his memory.

"I was 14 at the time my father died. He was a happy man, very compassionate, always helping others. Everyone who knew him would come to me and say I was like my father. I said no, but I want to be like him. He was someone I always looked up to, and I've tried to live my life the way he would have wanted. I think about my father every day. After his death I wasn't the same, till that moment I was a happy kid and my family was very united; from then I became a different person. Something like that affects you, it has to. Afterwards I dreamed of my dad working outside on a secret mission because it would relieve me of not accepting the reality.

"The influence of my dad was no longer with me, and I didn't feel like asking my mother how things worked; you know, just normal questions about puberty, maturity, and male things that only my father would be able to answer. It wasn't that I didn't ask my mother because I didn't trust her, I just felt embarrassed. I knew that if I asked her these kinds of questions it would only remind her of my dad."

Carlos has followed in his father's footsteps, not only working at INDER, but from a personal perspective as well.

"I like to travel, to meet other people. I like the political, the interchange of ideas. In my job at INDER I have the opportunity to meet people from around the world. Cuba is well known for amateur sports and many teams and individuals come here to study our sports system, to train with us. And so I have the opportunity to meet many of these people. Now, however, things are slower for us, because of the economic problems we face. We don't have as many sports exchanges as before."

The subject turns to the exact day Carlos found out about the explosion. He is sitting at his kitchen table and his speech and hand movements become more animated, more intense.

"I was in the military academy, I was 14 years old, studying in secondary school. My mother went to the airport to wait for my father.

She was told the airplane had an accident. That's what they said, that's all they knew at the time. Communication was bad back then and there was little information. So she went to the sports center building where the president of INDER said the plane went into the sea. It was a hit, a very violent strike for all of us to hear that.

"The day my father died, he was 39. And you know, it's funny, but when I was 38 years old and was close to turning 39 I started to panic. You asked why? That's how the mind works, thinking that the same thing could possibly happen to me, and I also have two young children and I had that in my mind for two or three years, emotionally it is very violent. I was always feeling panic. It was something you can't imagine. I'm 45 years old now, but there's still a little bit of that still with me.

"The bombing of Cubana Airlines was the bloodiest act of terrorism against Cuba. It hurt the whole country. But for those who have been directly affected by it, it's worse. It's with you always. It's constantly talked about in Cuba. Everyone knows and there is always something on the radio, on the television, some notice about it. You can never get away from it."

Carlos turns his thoughts away from his father to the subject of terrorism.

"When you talk about this to Cubans, it's not a political subject. The situation for many of us is different but at the same time if you talk to any Cuban about this incident they don't understand how someone can put two bombs in an airplane, it's a very irrational thing. The millions of Cubans that participated in the funeral felt what we were feeling, there was no political tone, they could be for or against the revolution but when you mention the Barbados the people don't have a different interpretation of what had happened. Everyone condemns it."

FELIPE QUINTERO DIAZ

At the time of the Cubana Airlines bombing, Felipe Quintero Diaz was the president of the Cuban Fencing Federation.

These days Felipe is retired, although still involved in various Cuban sports organizations. He lives in a well kept detached home in the Siboney district of Havana. The conversation is conducted on his outdoor patio connected to the side of the house. It is an open air courtyard with a tin roof, plenty of plants and a boisterous cockatoo in a small cage.

Felipe Quintero Diaz

Since the bombing Felipe has lived with the knowledge that but for the fortune of logistics and fate, he would have been on that plane. And that his best friend Manuel Permuy would have lived.

"I was initially assigned to go to the competition in Venezuela. I was going to help co-ordinate some sports agreements between Venezuela and the Havana City sports directory. It had to do with arrangements with the Central America competition. Not just for fencing, but for many other sports.

"But as it turned out I didn't go to Venezuela. Even though I was the president of the Cuban Fencing Federation, it was decided that three officials didn't need to go, for economic reasons, and two would be sufficient. So it was decided to send [Manuel] Permuy for the contracts.

If all these agreements weren't going to be signed, I'd have gone and Permuy would have stayed home."

The Venezuelan tournament was a stepping stone to the Olympics, and the Cuban team had one goal in mind.

"The objective was for Cuba to win all the gold medals. Yes, I knew most of the fencers personally, it was a good group, enthusiastic and dedicated. When the tournament finished we did win all the gold medals. It was October 6 in the afternoon and we were making these preparations to welcome them at the airport. I received a call from the INDER president, so I go to the office, without having any idea what I would be told. My first reaction after finding out was that it was only a minor accident. I thought maybe there was an accident on the airstrip, but after further discussion I was informed there was a bomb that exploded on the plane, it still had to be confirmed but it looked that way.

"Imagine how I felt, I felt very bad. When one thinks of the motivation to kill, to commit this act of terrorism, there is no way to feel the depth of the outrage, of the hate—it's inexplicable."

Reluctantly, Felipe confronts the question that has haunted him for more than 30 years.

"Many times, this question is always on my mind—why did I live while those others died? In the final idea I don't know what is better—to live or to be on that plane with Permuy. Sometimes I feel I should have been in his place. But the life is as it is—you have to accept life as it comes. When we face these problems we overcome the difficulties. And it became even more important to work harder and recover the fencing team, it took us many years to reach the level of expertise we had before. The bombing was a cruel act, it was a huge blow against Cuba."

MARTA HERNÁNDEZ HERNÁNDEZ

The sprawling town of Cotorro lies approximately 45 minutes outside Havana. The long bustling streets are filled with all modes of street transportation available in Cuba; pedestrians, bikers, buses, cars and trucks and various types of horse drawn conveyances. Cotorro is known for Cuba's largest and most important steel factory, located just a few minutes from the town square.

Marta Hernández Hernández

Marta Hernández Hernández is a gracious, thin woman who looks much younger than her 76 years. In Cuba Marta is often described as a *Fina*, an elderly lady with fine manners and sophisticated etiquette. It is a description of respect. She owns a small farm, a *finca*, where she grows various vegetables, raises pigs and chickens. Mango trees surround the house. She lives with her son and daughter-in-law. Marta worked for years as a cashier, she is now retired.

Like most victims of the Cubana Airlines bombing, she remembers the event as if it happened last week. With her is a copy of the book, *Ni olvidados, ni muertos* (Neither unforgotten, nor dead). The work is a bibliographical history of each member of the Cuban fencing team who lost their life in the bombing, as well as background information on the other Cuban sports officials on the plane. She refers to the edition a number of times, calling attention to her son's picture and description of his fencing achievements. It is an obvious comfort to her and throughout the interview she opens and closes it constantly. "It helps me connect to my son," she explains. It also appears to give her strength to continue speaking of the event that cost the life of her child.

"I've lived in Cotorro for more than 40 years. My son was a member of the fencing team—his name was Candido Munoz Fernandez. He became involved in fencing, and I remember he was starting to study to become a veterinarian, he loved animals. But it was very demanding, these studies, and he was not able to devote as much time as he wanted to the sport, but he was still very good at it.

"From the time he was a young boy he loved playing. One day he asked his father to make him a wooden sword, and he would play with that always. So it was natural for him to get involved in fencing. It's not a normal sport for most Cubans, they like to play baseball, or basketball, but he always loved fencing.

"At the time of Barbados it was his sixth, I think sixth, international competition." She checks the book for confirmation of her son's record. It's established that her son competed in nine international tournaments. "In Venezuela he was still a member of the junior team, he was being trained to become a part of the national team in a few years. He was part of the Equipo de Florete [foil] where he won a gold medal.

"He was a very friendly boy, he and the other members would come here to my house and spend the weekend, I was the mother to the whole team. My son would always say to them when they were leaving; 'kiss mom.' He loved to play with the children and he'd always have that wooden sword—he'd come into the kitchen and attack me with it," Marta smiles and lets out a subdued laugh, rapidly moving her gaze to the others in the room. She remembers painfully how the news came to her.

"I knew the plane was delayed, and then I don't know how long after, was it a few hours, or the next day? It had to be the next day. Someone knocked on the door, it was my brother, he advised me that there was an accident on the plane, there was some problem. But I knew, I had a feeling that it was much worse. After, I don't know, I don't remember what happened after, I was very confused. All the relatives came over, the street was full of people, everyone knew but no one wanted to tell me exactly what happened. He was very much loved.

"Three days later I knew what really happened. In the Plaza de la Revolución there was a big speech, millions of people were there. I was still in a bad state, I was unconscious so much of the time then. But I forced myself to get out of bed and go to the funeral, I had to gather my strength. You can't imagine what it was like, it wasn't real, I was in a very bad condition, I had a nervous breakdown and everyone was trying to comfort me.

"I'm still very nervous, I don't like to remember, I'm still not well. The anniversary of the bombing, every October, it affects me still. For Cubans it is something to remember, but for me it's different, I live it every day."

3
Hotel Bombings

In the years following the disintegration of the Soviet Union in 1989, Cuba suffered through what was called the Special Period, a time of economic hardship that saw the nation's GDP drop by more than 40 percent as a result of the collapse of its prime trading partner. From 1990 to 1994 Cuban production fell by one third, imports and exports were reduced by almost two thirds.

In looking for ways to recover, the government decided upon a number of measures, including a move towards opening up the under-developed tourist industry. By the mid 1990s a string of new hotels appeared in Havana, many along the north coast in the Miramar neighborhood. The hotels attracted not only waves of tourists from Europe and Canada, but also increasing numbers of businessmen looking to negotiate joint ventures with the more flexible elements of the Cuban government. Along with the new construction, efforts were made to upgrade existing establishments including Havana's signature hotel, the Nacional. At the same time dozens of all-inclusive resorts were springing up in the famous beach area of Varadero, 90 minutes east of the city. The new focus was reaping immediate benefits, and soon tourism was developing into the country's most important economic sector, more so than even the traditional sugar exports.

With the sightseers and businessmen came another wave—of terrorist bombings that targeted more than a dozen hotels and tourist spots from

April to September 1997. The campaign resulted in dozens injured and the death of an Italian tourist.

Hotel Nacional

Prior to the bombings there had been an attack targeting the Melia hotel in Varadero on October 7, 1992. There were also numerous threats against those who wanted to travel to the island. In late 1993 Canadian newspapers reported on Alpha 66 warnings, "...the anti-Castro terrorist group Alpha 66 announced that it now considered tourists in Cuba as justifiable targets for kidnappings and assassinations. Since Canadian tourists make up the largest single group of tourists in Cuba...it is clear that we constitute the largest probable target."[1]

A year later Alpha 66 announced in Florida that several of its commandos attacked a hotel on the northern coast, marking the start of a campaign against the tourist industry. "All the Cuban tourist centers are military objectives for Alpha 66," said the group's military chief, Humberto Pérez. The attacks were co-ordinated in Miami, he added.[2]

The 1997 bombing campaign was carried out by a group of Salvadorians, allegedly recruited and paid for by Luis Posada Carriles.

Posada, long known for his anti-Castro activities, had traveled to Salvador with the intent of hiring nationals to carry out the hotel bombings, according to Cuban prosecutors during the 1999 trial of one of those charged with setting the bombs. Posada connected directly with two of the Salvadorians: Francisco Chávez Abarca and Otto René Rodríguez Llerena. Abarca was a subordinate who had previous dealings with Posada. A third individual, Raúl Ernesto Cruz León, was hired by Chávez Abarca through Posada. Of the three, Cruz León became the most infamous. Details of the campaign were corroborated by Posada himself in a series of newspaper interviews conducted a year later. In a *New York Times* article Posada acknowledged involvement in the Havana hotel bombings, commenting, "We didn't want to hurt anybody."[3] Subsequent to that interview he has denied any link to those attacks. At the time of the interview he stated he was financed by the Cuban American National Foundation, referring to former president Jorge Mas Canosa: "Jorge controlled everything, each time I needed money he asked someone to send me 5,000 dollars, 10,000 dollars, 15,000 dollars."[4]

Additional verification of his involvement surfaced from Enrique Bernales Ballesteros, the United Nations Human Rights Commission Special Rapporteur, who visited Havana in September 1999 to investigate the bombings. His subsequent report outlined the details of the campaign and the connection Posada had with the accused.

Ballesteros's visit was based on an invitation from the Cuban government contained in a January 1999 UN report where the Cubans told Ballesteros: "Otto René Rodríguez admitted that he had caused the explosion that took place on 4 July 1997 in the lobby of the Cohiba Hotel in Havana and that he had been recruited, trained and supplied by Luis Posada Carriles, a terrorist of Cuban origin, who had paid him around US$1,000 for that action. He stated that, on this occasion, too, his motive was financial and that it was once again Posada Carriles who had supplied the components and financed the trip.

"Given that these operations are linked with Miami-based extremist organizations, as Posada Carriles himself admitted in his *New York Times* interview, the Government of Cuba once again urged the Special Rapporteur to use his good offices to request the United States authorities to take firm and decisive action to put an end to these objectionable activities."[5]

The first of the series of bombs exploded in the bathroom of the Ache disco in Havana's newly opened Hotel Meliá Cohiba on April 12, 1997. Chávez Abarca, who was found to be in Cuba three times from April to May of that year, was later identified as the person responsible. The second Salvadorian, Otto René Rodríguez, planted one bomb at the same Cohiba hotel on July 1997, and was subsequently arrested in June 1998 while attempting to bring in components for two explosive devices. The third Salvadorian ended up planting at least six of the deadliest bombs. Ernesto Cruz León was recruited by Chávez Abarca, who convinced him to carry out a series of terrorist missions in Cuba. One of the bombs went off at the Hotel Copacabana, killing Fabio Di Celmo. A former member of El Salvador's military, Cruz León was 26 when he was recruited and trained. Cruz León later testified he never met Posada, but knew of him through his contact with Chávez Abarca, who spoke of Posada often.

León revealed he was to be paid approximately US$2,000 for each bomb detonated. He was provided with a list of hotels, and given flexibility as to where and when the explosives would be placed. Cruz León claimed he was hesitant at first, reluctant to be responsible for any deaths or injuries. Chávez Abarca reportedly responded to his concern by saying: "Well, try to put it in the lobby in a place where you won't kill anybody, but if there are people that die, that's the price. If there are people that die, they die."[6] Following his arrest in September 1997, Cruz León was given the death sentence, later commuted. While awaiting trial, Posada expressed little sympathy over Cruz León's arrest or his fate. "He's not Cuban," Posada said dismissively to a *Miami Herald* newspaper reporter in 1998. "He did this for money."[7]

Posada then went on to describe Cruz León as a mercenary, confirming he had been working for him, but said that "maybe a dozen" others reporting to him remained at large. Cruz León and the others were given full instructions on how to bring the various bomb parts through Cuban customs. The C-4 plastic explosives were smuggled in bottles of White Rain and Prell shampoo, or in the soles of black leather boots. Fixed with adhesive tape to digital clocks, detonators and 9-volt batteries, they became powerful explosives.

The bombings that began at the disco in the Meliá Cohiba moved quickly on to the Capri, Nacional, Varadero's Sol Palmeras, Tritón, Chateau-Miramar and the Copacabana, all between April and September 1997. Most of these hotels were situated in the same waterfront neighborhood in north Havana. A bomb planted at the Comodoro Hotel in the same northern coastal area failed to explode, thanks to the unintentional intervention of a young and curious Cuban chess player.

Along with the hotels, Cuba's most famous restaurant/bar, La Bodeguita del Medio, had its second floor torn apart from one of Cruz León's bombs. A number of other explosives were found before detonating, including one at Havana's José Marti international airport, and another one on a tourist mini bus. For his part in the campaign Posada attempted to backtrack on his admissions of masterminding the plan. He had no such hesitations when he gave an interview to the *New York Times* on July 12, 1998 when he described the Italian tourist's death as a freak accident, but he declared that he had a clear conscience, saying, "I sleep like a baby. It is sad that someone is dead, but we can't stop." He added, "That Italian was sitting in the wrong place at the wrong time."[8]

GIUSTINO DI CELMO

Giustino Di Celmo does not look 87 years old. He has a short, sturdy build, a round face with few wrinkles. He walks steadily without assistance and possesses a firm, responsive handshake. When questioned on his longevity, without hesitation he produces identification to prove his age. As he comments wryly, there are not many others of his age that compare with his physical condition. "Because there's not many my age around anymore," he laughs. His work, he says, keeps him alive.

Giustino Di Celmo

Giustino is the father of Fabio, the beloved son who was killed at the Hotel Copacabana during the series of bomb explosions that hit the Havana hotels. Fabio was killed by the merest of chance, when a tiny shard of glass struck him in the jugular vein. Another few centimeters and he would not have died. Fabio was the only fatality during the succession of detonations that went off during those months of 1997.

Following Fabio's death Giustino decided to move permanently to Cuba, with the purpose of opening a restaurant and name it after his son. Although most of his time is spent in Havana, he still takes the opportunity for visits back to his Italian homeland as well as to his other residence in Canada.

His head is that of a capitalist, but he has a socialist heart, Giustino laughs.

"I opened the restaurant in 2005 and named it Fabio. After he died, the Cuban government asked me what were Fabio's dreams—he had two dreams: to bring his soccer team in Genoa, Italy to come play in Cuba; his second dream was to open a restaurant here.

"He was a big soccer fanatic, he loved to play the game. But all his friends who played soccer in Italy asked him if there were good Italian restaurants in Cuba, that they wouldn't come unless they could go to a good pizzeria. I told this to the Cuban government and they agreed to help me fulfill Fabio's dreams.

"Fabio was killed in the Hotel Copacabana in 1997—in 1998 Fabio's soccer team came to Cuba to play some exhibition games. It was Fabio's dream come true, it was mine as well."

He is unreserved in his condemnation of terrorism, and what it can do to the soul of those left behind.

"This is very important, I've said this to the world press. Terrorism is an endless monster, each victim of terrorism—the parents want revenge. I wanted revenge as well and maybe I would have achieved it had it not been for the Cuban Revolution—Fidel said not to seek revenge.

"In this moment when I am talking to you—what time is it? It's 6:12 p.m. In three hours it will be dark here, and in this time 20,000 children will have died from hunger around the world. Twenty thousand corpses because they don't have a piece of bread to eat. But not one of those 20,000 who will die of hunger lives in Cuba."

He speaks softly of his son and the type of person he was, and the day he died. "Fabio was an entrepreneur, he was a businessman like me, he traveled all over Latin America. He didn't know Cuba much, but when he came here he fell in love with Cuba. I was doing business here since 1992, my son started coming in 1994.

"He was 32 years old when he died. At first he had no political ideas, he was too young. Then in 1994 he asked me how is it possible in this country, this poor country, there are no children barefoot, no children who go hungry. I told him of the system here, the socialist system, and then Fabio said 'I want to be a socialist.' He had such a connection with the people."

Besides his love of Cuba, Fabio's other passion was soccer, Giustino says. "Fabio organized a football team in each neighborhood in Havana. These teams are still playing. Fabio bought a trophy for the club that would win the tournament. He played for Miramar [the neighborhood in Havana where the hotel was located], and that side won the first Havana championship. The players on the team wanted to give Fabio the trophy, but he wouldn't accept it, the cup is now in a museum in Havana. There's a room in the museum, room number five, dedicated to Fabio." The Museo de la Marcha del Pueblo Combatiente is located in Playa Municipality on Avenue 13 and 70.

"Fabio—I never say he passed away, I say he went away, because in many ways he's still with me. He had an impact in Cuba, he was an exceptional person. One day in Havana he saw a young boy crying, he asked what happened and the boy told him he had his bike stolen—that he just went upstairs to his apartment for five minutes and he came back and his bike was stolen. The boy was so distressed because he said he didn't know how he would be able to tell his dad—his dad would be very upset. So Fabio took the boy and brought him to a store and bought him a new bike. That's how love is expressed."

Giustino is asked if he ever thinks, why Fabio? He pauses for a few moments, responding in a soft, slow voice.

"I think of that question every night. I'm Catholic. A person like Fabio, no one can live in this world. I think God needed him and that's why he took him away. Every night I think of Fabio, and ask, why him? That little piece that killed him, the fate of that. I'm sure he called out to me and I couldn't do anything."

The death of his son has cemented his resolve to struggle against what he considers to be America's iniquitous policies towards the Cuba people.

"When Fabio died I took the decision to fight against terrorism, and to get involved wherever you see injustice. To consider these killers, when I think of them, I want justice. The worst act of terrorism was the bombing of the Cubana Airlines. The two who planted the bomb, they declared in court, international court, the process of bombing the plane, the ones who financed the act, the masterminds. [Luis] Posada is the result of all this injustice.

"The United States government has for the past 50 years been torturing Cuba, why? This country is no military threat. The only difference is the system. If you build hospitals, if you build schools, if you eliminate unemployment and hunger, for this you are attacked, for this you are subjected to terrorism? No one in the United States knows about this, these terrorist attacks against Cuba, they only know the bad things."

CHANG ALVAREZ ALVO

Picking up the small, tightly wrapped object found on the far side of the short concrete barrier near the hotel's outdoor pool, Chang Alvarez Alvo did what any normal 13-year-old would do; he invited his friends over for an impromptu game of soccer. The four boys played with the package for a few minutes, then became bored. Fortunate, as the object they were so carelessly kicking could have exploded at any moment, and with the amount of plastic C-4 it contained would have blown them to bits, along with dozens of others.

Chang Alvarez Alvo

Chang, a quiet, introspective young man, had no idea that what he had retrieved at the Comodoro Hotel was one of the bombs planted by

Raúl Ernesto Cruz León, the most famous of the bombers who were terrorizing Cuban tourist spots during the spring and summer of 1997.

The Comodoro was a natural target. It was one in the series of hotels located on the north coast of Havana. Known for catering to tour groups and businessmen, the hotel was famous for an outstanding view of the ocean and a popular disco. The Comodoro is located just down the road from the Copacabana, where Fabio Di Celmo was killed from an explosion set by León.

For Chang, the package he found simply represented an unexpected amusement, something to occupy himself as he waited for his turn at the national chess tournament being held at the hotel. The event attracted hundreds of players and their parents, and Chang, eleven years later, reflects on the devastation that could have been wrought that day.

"If the bomb had gone off when we were kicking it around it would have killed a lot of people, including me," he says with a small smile. Chang demonstrates an easy sense of humor, and irony.

He remembers the day vividly, not only for coming across the deadly package.

"It was in April, 1977 and I was at the hotel for the chess tournament. The meet was for Cuban players of different ages and skill levels, it was a national tournament. As a child I really liked playing chess, I started playing in primary school, maybe it was around fifth grade. After that I went to scholarship school [a post secondary education institution where Cubans with exceptional talent are identified and given the opportunity to hone their skills].

"When I found the bomb it was about the third or fourth day of the tournament. There were some other friends with me and we were all waiting to go into the hotel for the competition. There was a big salon set aside for it, big enough to hold hundreds of people.

"At the hotel where we were all standing, there was a little grassy area, which was edged by a short concrete wall and some electrical cables and outlets. This area was close to the outdoor swimming pool.

There was a glass door that led into the hotel, also close to the area, and which separated the meeting rooms from one another.

"On the grass was a package, just lying there. It was tightly wrapped in toilet paper and plastic and covered in tape." Chang holds out his hands to show the dimensions of the package, about six inches across and three or four inches high. The approximate size and shape of a soccer ball.

"So I looked at it, not too closely, took it over to my friends, we tossed it in the air a few times, and then we started kicking it to each other. It was very tightly wrapped, nothing came undone from the kicking.

"After a few minutes we got bored. I became curious to know what was inside it, so I opened it up. I removed the paper and nylon and I saw all this plastic material inside—it was soft and easy to mold. I pushed my fingers into this plastic and removed as much of it as I could, to see what was under it. I took the plastic out and tossed it on the ground, on the grassy area of the hotel."

It was a considerable time later that Chang realized he was removing the C-4 explosive, about two pounds worth, an action he's convinced saved his life and hundreds of others at least twice during the next few hours.

"After taking most of the plastic out I saw there was a calculator, with a 9-volt battery, with some wires and stuff. There was this little watch attached as well. It was a Casio watch, black. I started to manipulate the watch, play with the calculator. Just to see if it worked, and it looked like it was working fine.

"I took out more of this plastic and I saw this little thing that was attached. I didn't realize what it was at the time, but when I got home later I looked at it and it said 'Explosive' on the side, it was in English, in blue letters. It was the detonator but at that time I didn't know what it was." He takes a deep breath and lets it out in a broad smile.

"I kept it all together, I thought it might be something useful but I didn't have time to examine it anymore, it was almost time to go into the hotel. But I was afraid my other friends would want parts of this thing, so I went to my mother and told her to put it into her handbag, I didn't want any of my friends playing with this, so for her to guard it for me. I played my chess games and then came out and went to my mom and asked her about this, to make sure my friends wouldn't come over and take it from me." At this confession Chang breaks out into a wide, sheepish grin. It is from a combination of embarrassment and relief.

"My mother did ask me about it—I just told her I found it and to put it in her bag. That's all I said about it. I was just a kid, who would have thought that it was a bomb? And my mother had no idea. Boy was she mad at me later when we found out. She couldn't believe what I brought home. But she didn't punish me, she knew I didn't know what it was—she didn't know what it was. No one did."

Now the grin turns into a short, deep laugh. "From the hotel my mom and I got onto a bus, we lived about 15 kilometers from the hotel. The bus was full, as it usually is, maybe 50 or more people on it. The road was very rough, there was a lot of bumping and moving around. And my mom still had this package in her purse. When we got home I told my family several times that this piece said 'Explosive' on the side, but no one paid attention to me, they thought I was joking."

Chang stops for a moment, collecting his thoughts on what might have happened, offering his opinion as to why the bomb didn't explode.

"I think maybe while I was kicking it the bomb became defused. Or maybe when I was playing with the watch and the calculator. But the most important thing I did, without knowing, was to take out the C-4 and throw it on the floor. Officials later told me that even with the C-4 out, if it had exploded it could have taken off my hand and caused damage to others. If the bomb still had all the C-4 and exploded in the hotel, or on the bus, it would have been horrible. Many would have died."

The package remained in his closet for almost two years before one night, "I was watching TV, and I saw this guy they were interviewing from El Salvador—I knew he was the one who put the bombs in hotels, he was being interviewed and they showed what his bombs looked like—and that's when I realized it was identical to what I had found. I went to school the next day and told my friends about it and my coach. They all laughed and said no way you found a bomb, they thought I was making it all up.

"The next week I took the parts to the school and showed them to my teachers and others, and then they said—yes—you did find a bomb. They weren't laughing anymore. The school officials notified the police and they came very fast to the school, they picked me up and collected my mom and we went to the hotel. They wanted to find the C-4, but they didn't find anything, this was two years later and there wasn't any trace of it around. They took my calculator from me, I wasn't too happy about that, and the next time I saw it was during the symbolic trial [the Cuban government televised a re-enactment of the trial of the bomber a few years after he was convicted]. Yes I miss it; I wish I still had the calculator."

He has little sympathy for the one who planted the bombs, or for those who masterminded the program.

"It was absolutely an act of terrorism, a lot of people could have died. I was at the hotel and there could have been hundreds killed if that bomb went off. There were so many people in the area at the time. I'm talking about if I hadn't found the bomb, and taken the C-4 out. What would have happened if I hadn't found the bomb, and it exploded?"

And if he ever comes across another strange package? "Next time I see a package on the street I'll just keep on walking," he laughs.

MARISOL VISOZO RAMIREZ

The Hotel Nacional opened on December 30, 1930 and is still considered to be Cuba's landmark hotel. The building rises over a spectacular view of the ocean and Havana's historic waterfront highway, the Malecón. The hotel is renowned for its classic Moorish-Spanish architecture, expansive gardens, and its main lobby resembling three parallel aisles of a Medieval church. The Nacional has hosted the world's rich and famous throughout its history, and played host to most of the infamous during Cuba's high crime days of the 1950s.

Marisol Visozo Ramirez

The Nacional was also the target of bomber Cruz León, who hid a deadly package under one of the large, comfortable leather sofas in the main lobby. It was there that Marisol Visozo Ramirez had the misfortune of meeting the Salvadorian.

"I was visiting a friend at the hotel. It was 1997, June or July. It was during the day around 10 a.m."

Marisol, 32, is visibly nervous talking about "the worst day of my life. I have such a hard time speaking of this, I hate it. I'm nervous about everything now. I was never this way before."

She struggles to continue. "When I entered the hotel I went left, in front of information desk, in the lobby. I met my friend and we spent about 30 minutes talking, everything was normal. I was with her and her husband. My friend, the woman, then went upstairs to get something. I stayed talking to her husband. At that time in the morning there were a lot of tourists in the lobby, they were waiting for the tour buses to pick them up and take them on their trips for the day. A lot of workers and tour guides were there as well. After a few minutes the tourists left, so the lobby was fairly empty at the time, maybe 20 or so people. My other friend left to get something, so I was sitting on the sofa by myself. After a few minutes this stranger sits by my side, to my left, at the end of the sofa. I was in the middle.

"He was a dark skinned man, I wasn't looking directly at him for any length of time. He was there just a few minutes. When he was about to leave, he stood up and asked me where the gallery was. I didn't know what he was taking about, so I told him I didn't know. [There is an art gallery located downstairs at the hotel.] Everything seemed normal about this person, I wasn't nervous, he didn't seem nervous, everything was calm.

"Two or three minutes later, no more than that, the bomb exploded. There was this tremendous noise, I didn't know what was happening. He had put the bomb on the side of the sofa, the same one I was sitting on. But the sofa saved my life. When the bomb exploded it must have absorbed most of the force. The explosion threw me to the floor, and the sofa was tossed away from me. At the time the bomb exploded I thought they wanted to kill me, that I was their target. Why? Who? I don't know, I've never done anything in my life, but that's what I was thinking.

"The bomb exploded, and I was knocked to the floor, I didn't feel any pain or anything, but the lobby was filling with smoke and dust. From the floor I saw people running all around, they ran out of the lobby, through these large windows. And I followed them." The hotel lobby opens out to a grand patio overlooking the oceanfront. Two giant wooden doors provide entrance to the courtyard, and either side is decorated with ceiling to floor windows.

"I knew the explosion took place from inside the lobby. I was bleeding from my ear, and I had a large deep cut on the left side of my face, my ear hurt. I think it was a piece of crystal, behind me there was a glass display case that shattered, it could have been from that. At that moment I thought I was dying."

Hotel damage during 1997 bombing campaign

After managing to make her way out to the terrace, Marisol was treated for her wounds.

"Once I was outside there were a lot of people running to the area, I was bleeding and a few came over to help me. Immediately I was put in a car and went to the Calixto Garcia hospital, about a kilometer away. The doctors there checked my face and stitched it up, and that was the first time I realized how bad I was cut. They put seven stitches. I still have the scar. I also had a burst ear drum. After the bombing when I was in the hospital I called my parents. My mother was more nervous than me, I had to calm her down. She was always afraid when I went out. And for me, every time I have to tell his story I become nervous. Whenever I see any documentary or news report on the bombings on TV, I turn it off, I don't want anything to do with him—ever."

Marisol admits she's had to seek psychiatric care to help her cope with the anxiety she continues to struggle with. "For many years I've been treated, but it doesn't help. It's something I have to deal with every day of my life. It happens often, one time I was at a disco, I saw some smoke come out like they do at these places and immediately I got scared that something was happening, that there was a bomb. I couldn't stay. I'm nervous all the time. It has affected my life completely."

She remembers details of the confession of Cruz León, including one important point the bomber left out.

"The last bomb he put was at La Bodeguita del Medio. When he left there he was arrested, the police knew who he was by then. But when he was confessing he didn't mention the one at the La Bodeguita, and it went off while they were interrogating him. How can you do something like that? I'll never be able to understand."

NICOLÁS RODRÍGUEZ VALDÉS

If the Nacional is the most famous hotel in Cuba, then La Bodeguita del Medio takes the title in the category of restaurant/bar.

This tiny tourist spot, located in the middle of Empedrado St. in Old Havana, has a long and illustrious history. La Bodeguita del Medio (Little Store in the Middle of the Street) started out as a grocery shop, which later became an eating establishment attracting local journalists. It wasn't long after that the rich and celebrated started frequenting the intimate surroundings, and now it is *the* spot for tourists to stop in for Havana's best *mojitos*—the rum-mint drink made famous by Ernest Hemingway. La Bodeguita has two floors, the main one always packed with visitors enjoying the drinks and the wall-filled photos of Hollywood stars and political celebrities. Upstairs is the dining area, serving traditional Cuban cuisine in two separate rooms.

The bomb in La Bodeguita was the last one placed by Cruz León, who had been arrested shortly after leaving the bar. When confessing to the Cuban authorities, he neglected to mention his handiwork on the upper level of the restaurant. The bomb exploded hours later.

The story of barman Nicolás Rodríguez Valdés, 41, includes an extensive interaction with the bomber and a remarkable photo that was taken of the two men.

Nicolás Rodríguez Valdés

"When the first bombs exploded in the hotels the authorities warned everyone working in tourist facilities to be on guard, no one knew where the next bomb would happen, which is what the terrorists wanted—they wanted everyone scared of going into hotels or bars, in order to destroy the Cuban tourist industry. La Bodeguita was always crowded. We had to watch everyone, to see if anyone was acting suspiciously, to see if there was any package that shouldn't be there, to always check the washrooms.

"One day everything seemed normal, except for one tourist. He came in and he went to the upper level, which is where I work. The upper level has two rooms—one large room and then another smaller one. This guy didn't want to use the large room, where a lot of people were, but he asked to be in the smaller room, where there was no one. When we served him his food he didn't eat hardly anything. So I thought he wasn't feeling well, I was the one serving him. But he looked nervous. I offered him a liquor, to maybe settle his stomach. Afterwards he went to the bathroom and I could hear him throwing up. I attended to him, took care of him and did my best to try and make him feel better.

"Then we spoke a few words and he took out his camera and asked if he could take a picture of him and me—he set his camera on automatic and took our picture. I was working the whole day; it was around 4 or 5 p.m. the first few days of September, 1997. I remember well because my son was born on August 26, just days before. A few hours after he left, there is a description of this person, as being the suspected bomber. Some witness at the Copacabana described him, and they passed this information on to the tourist places.

"Immediately I notified the manager of this guy who was here, this was a very serious situation. By this time it was around 9 p.m. I was confident it was the same person who was here. By this time he had been arrested and started to confess to all the bombs he had placed in the different hotels. A manager and co-worker went to the police to identify him, I stayed at La Bodeguita.

"I closed the upper part of the bar, where he had been, but the lower part was left open. So all the people from the upper part had to move down to the lower, which made the lower part more crowded. I was in the upper part preparing some papers and closing the bar when suddenly—boom!!—I heard the explosion. There was a showcase in that room where we'd sell souvenirs, as well as a freezer where the beer and other beverages were stored. He had placed the bomb behind the freezer. It shattered the showcase and tore off a large part of the floor. And the table he was sitting at before, along with the floor, fell down to the lower level. There was a group of four Mexicans sitting at a table on the lower level, and the table and chairs and floor from the upper level came crashing down on them. Luckily no one was hurt.

"I was about two or three meters from the freezer when the bomb went off. The bomb exploded and everything turned black from the smoke and dust—I couldn't see anything. I had no idea what was going on and I was afraid that there might be another bomb. So I jumped over the bar and made my way down the stairs. I couldn't hear anything as both my ears were blown out."

While Nicolás had no explanation why the whole bar wasn't evacuated while they were looking for the bomb, he does remember vividly the chaos of the lower level.

"It was mass confusion downstairs, people were screaming and crying and trying to get out as fast as they could. This is a small bar, and the door is narrow, so people were pushing and shoving to get out. It was total panic. But everyone got out without anyone suffering serious injuries. It was incredible. No one could understand what was happening. The police arrived immediately and investigators shortly afterwards.

"I think I was the most affected because I was the closest. I still can't hear from my right ear. No one was hurt bad but if there had been people on the upper floor when the bomb went off they would have been killed. The room was completely destroyed. The windows were shattered and the glass fell on the house beside the bar. And if the bomb had gone off on the bottom level... I can't imagine what would have happened, the amount of destruction that would have caused.

"When he was captured he didn't even mention the Bodeguita bomb, in order to cover himself. But the bomb went off when he was in police custody. That son of a bitch. The next day I went to the police office to identify him, and as soon as I saw him I said that's the guy. He is a monster, there are no words to describe him.

"I was off work for one month for my medical problems. I've never recovered my hearing in the one ear. But more than the physical damage, something like this creates psychological damage, it affects you for the rest of your life. You can't ever escape from it. Every time I see someone with a package I react to it. And every day tourists bring in packages, many times tourists come in and leave packages, they forget them. Every time that happens I feel it again, in the pit of my stomach, that same fear. All the time."

Nicolás continues to tend the bar at La Bodeguita, and has obtained a certain level of fame for his experience with the bomber. Tourists come and ask for the barman who met the bomber, and they point to him as he tells the same story, time after time.

He says he'd like to have the picture the bomber took of the two together, just to look at his face and try to understand why he did it. But more important than the photo, which he says he'd put up on the bar wall, is his professional reputation at La Bodeguita.

"I make the best *mojitos* at La Bodeguita," he laughs loudly. "But don't ask anyone else who works there, because they'd say the same thing."

4

Operation Peter Pan

Copies of the official looking document were passed out surreptitiously to the congregation. Catholic priests gave instructions not to divulge where the information came from, only to understand what this new law meant, and then notify as many others as quickly as possible. The details spread like wildfire among the middle and upper classes, bringing horror along the way.

The priests said the handout was indisputable proof of what the new revolutionary government was planning. Known as the Apócrifa—or La Patria Potestad, the Act of Parental Authority—this single piece of paper purported to legalize the state's intention of usurping parental control. It would soon drive thousands of mothers and fathers to send their young to a foreign land.

The document outlined how the government would take control of the children, and the lengthy jail term for those who disobeyed. At the bottom appeared the names of Dr. Fidel Castro Ruiz, Prime Minister and Dr. Osvaldo Dorticós Torrado, President of the Republic. These were the two most powerful political figures in Cuba at the time the certificate was dated, August 31, 1961. There was no doubt this was the law that would transfer parental authority to the state. Children would be torn from their homes; parents would have no say in how their offspring were to be raised. It was a convincing piece of paper, examined without hesitation or suspicion. Few who read it did not believe, and fewer still noticed the lack of signatures or government seals.

Cuban church officials knew, however, that what they were handing out was a lie. As did the Roman Catholic Diocese in Miami, along with the various State Department officers in America and the network of CIA agents in Havana who were all accused by the Cuban government of working on this elaborate deception. The Act of Parental Authority was a fabrication. Officials had no interest or intention in removing parental authority. This was all just a calculated scheme to discredit the government and instill psychological terrorism upon Cuba's religious faithful.

It was extremely effective. The program, eventually to become known as Operation Peter Pan, led to the exodus of more than 14,000 children from November 1960 to October 1962. The vast majority of these young Cubans were taken in by Miami Church organizations. When the American part of the program was shut down due to the cancellation of flights after the Cuban Missile Crisis of October 1962, efforts were switched to take children out to Spain and other countries. Experts on Operation Peter Pan say remnants of the program continued on until 1981. In total, the program was estimated to have affected more than 25,000 children. The majority came from parents who lived in the cities—Havana in particular. While the normal age of a Peter Pan ranged from five to 16, infants and older teenagers were also spirited out. A number of babies arrived at Miami with no documents, ending up in orphanages with no chance of ever finding their real parents.

The collaborators went further than just printing up and distributing the fake document. Church executives and their ecclesiastical supporters knocked on hundreds of doors in an effort to speak personally to parents about this frightening new decree. Parents with children attending Catholic schools were specifically targeted. To add to the horror, mothers were told that if they didn't surrender their children they'd be subject to 15 years in jail, or simply made to disappear. At the same time a propaganda campaign was claiming the Cuban government was torturing Church administrators. Fortunately, those supposedly being abused denounced these slanderous radio announcements, originating from Radio Swan, the CIA controlled radio station off the coast of Honduras. Radio Swan was created by the CIA in May 1960 under the direction of one of the most influential officials specializing in psychological warfare, David Atlee Phillips. It was Radio Swan that broadcast the initial Peter Pan propaganda in October of that year: "Mothers listen to this, the next government law will be to take away all those children from five to 18 years old from their mothers. Cuban mothers don't let your son be taken away from you. The new government law is to take your children away at five years old and give them back to you when he is 18 years. And by then he will already be a monster. Attention mothers, go to church and follow instructions from the clergy."[1]

The lies even traveled to other countries, with a lurid 1961 newspaper ad in Costa Rica warning parents not to let their children suffer the same fate as those in Cuba. The propaganda came with a shocking picture of a Cuban military official grabbing a child while the mother screamed helplessly in the background.

The conspirators were able to effectively combine the propaganda lies with actual government programs taking place at the same time. When the Cuban government handed out forms for working women to fill out in order to determine how many day care centers needed to be created, Peter Pan organizers used that as proof of the Apócrifa.

Operation Peter Pan was aimed at the most important aspect of Cuban society—the family. It was directed at the bourgeoisie, the financial class with the most to lose under the revolution. It played upon the anxiety these people already had of the economic and social changes taking place, and manipulated those fears in order to strangle the middle and upper classes into panic. For the less sophisticated the methods were cruder; they were told the Cuban government was going to send their children to the Soviet Union to make sausages out of them. A common tactic was to convince parents that the revolution

Alerta Costarricense!

Esto está pasando en CUBA...
No permita que suceda AQUI!

> Los canallas al servicio de la tiranía comunista de Cuba hoy, llegan a los hogares y le quitan a la madre los hijos para llevarlos a escuelas del estado en donde les enseñan a no creer en Dios, ni en la familia, ni en los padres. Hay casos de niños indoctrinados que han llegado al colmo de delatar a sus padres y de enviarlos al paredón.

Para llegar a este nefasto sistema, hubo en Cuba una pequeña minoría comunista que trabajaba, igual que aquí, en forma clandestina y que no se echaba de ver.

Los camaradas ticos son idénticos a los de Cuba, Hungría y China... trabajan... trabajan y trabajan solapadamente esperando algún día vender el país a la conspiración internacional.

POR LA PAZ
CON PROGRESO Y LIBERTAD!

Alerta costarricense! Hágase Vigilante Democrático y denuncie a los camaradas ticos y sus amigos a los ιιιtordcrfes o al

C.V.D.-36-2

COMITE DE VIGILANCIA DEMOCRATICA
Un movimiento desligado de la política electoral
Apartado 5068   San José

Costa Rican newspaper advertisement, January 1961: "Costa Ricans Alert! This is happening in Cuba... don't let it happen here!"

73

would last only a few months, that the Americans would come in and sweep Fidel and his socialism aside, and for safety's sake parents should send their children away while all this went down. The result was the abandonment of thousands of children who had no concept as to why they were being torn from their family. On the parents' side, the misplaced faith they placed in the Church meant many would never see their children again.

Two of the principals behind Operation Peter Pan were Father Bryan O. Walsh and James Baker. Monsignor Walsh was the director of the Catholic Welfare Bureau in Miami. The legend goes that a Cuban boy by the name of Pedro Menendez was sent to the United States in the early months of 1960 but was unable to find a place to stay. A Cuban refugee eventually brought Pedro to Walsh asking for assistance. Walsh took pity on the boy and decided to arrange shelter through the church and it was from Pedro that he got the idea to set up an operation to bring Cuban children out and house them through the church.[2]

Walsh moved to bring Cuban children out through a disinformation program, which was met with the active support from the United States government. It was decided that the plan to arrange exit visas under Walsh's direction would be co-ordinated through the State Department, and a system was set up that offered funds to the Catholic Welfare Bureau for every Cuban brought out, allegedly adding up to millions of dollars. Walsh organized the facilities at his Catholic Welfare Bureau to house the Cuban children, as well as arranging locations in foster homes or other locations for those his organization couldn't handle. From Operation Peter Pan Walsh eventually became the architect of the infamous Cuban Adjustment Act of 1966, which to this day gives Cubans landing on American soil fast track eligibility for residency after one year. Opponents of this Act say it encourages illegal immigration, resulting in Cubans trying, and dying, to reach the United States on unsafe rafts or through unscrupulous human traffickers. No other country outside of Cuba has this immigration advantage.

The details of the Operation came out during the final years of Walsh's life when he spoke of his relationship with Baker, the State Department and the CIA in connection with Peter Pan.[3]

In Cuba, James Baker was the point man. Headmaster of Ruston Academy, an American school in Havana, Baker was working independently on ways to get a few of his charges out of Cuba when he met up with Walsh. The pair connected in late 1960 to discuss how they could work together. Both parts meshed perfectly—Walsh would supply the visas, Baker would provide the children.

Once Operation Peter Pan was up and running, Baker was given the authority to distribute I-20 student visas issued by Walsh through the State Department. While the I-20 visas were effective, it was decided a more comprehensive waiver visa would be more appropriate. These visas were approved by the State Dept on January 9, 1961 and an estimated 50,000 were handed out until October 1962. The process violated every American immigration law at that time.

With hundreds leaving Cuba weekly under these visas, the CIA decided to take over direct sponsorship of the program in July 1961. Top CIA planners apparently decided Operation Peter Pan would be a perfect way to discredit the Cuban government and sow dissent and terror among the population. While the State Department has admitted its role in the operation, the CIA has steadfastly refused to acknowledge its participation, citing security reasons. Finally, in the mid 1980s declassified American government documents revealed the extent of CIA involvement.[4]

In 1961 Baker left Cuba to work directly under Walsh. Before leaving, Walsh named brother and sister Ramón and Pola Grau to take over Baker's responsibilities in the Operation. The two Cubans were ardent anti-Castro activists with suspected deep connections to the CIA. The Graus supplied Walsh with the names of the children to be taken out and with the distribution of the visas. Years afterwards in a *Miami Herald* interview, Ramón, known as Groucho, admitted his participation in Operation Peter Pan and the CIA connection.

In a November 1990 edition of the paper he commented that it was politics that drove the American government's involvement in Peter Pan. "The entire thing was a propaganda test to hurt Fidel," he was quoted in the article, and the idea was to create panic, with the hope it would foster unrest and rebellion against the Cuban regime.[5]

Pola Grau later described Operation Peter Pan as child abuse, and confirmed the American government's participation was not humanitarian, pointing to the incident in the 1980s where the State Department turned down a request from the United Nations High Commissioner for Refugees to help reunite the Cuban children with their parents.

Ramón and Pola were eventually caught and convicted for their connections with the CIA, espionage and attempting to overthrow the Castro government. Both were sentenced in 1966 to 30 years in prison. Neither one was ever charged for their part in Operation Peter Pan. In fact no person was ever arrested or tried, except for those who printed the false law.

Pola Grau was released in 1978, her brother in 1986. Both returned to Miami immediately after release. While in prison Pola wrote extensively on her involvement in Operation Peter Pan. It was from these papers that the Cuban government finally realized the extent of the program.

Along with the Graus and Baker, dozens of CIA agents and American officials still in Cuba were accused of continuing to work the operation. Just as important was the support of the two airlines that flew the children out of Havana—Pan Am and KLM. These were the only carriers who participated in the American part of the program, and were alleged to have altered passenger lists to expedite the removal of the youngsters, according to one of the leading experts on Operation Peter Pan, Ramón Torreira Crespo.

Ramón, co-author of the history of Operation Peter Pan, described during an interview at his Havana apartment how well thought out and implemented the process was.

"It operated right under the noses of the government. The concept began when planners realized how easy it was to get Cuban children out of the country under the I-20 visas. Arrangements of these visas were partially based on a Cuban youth proving he was registered in an American university or post secondary institution. With that, the visa was easy to obtain. So the Peter Pan organizers used this to get hold of these visas, with the full support of the American side."

Ramón Torreira Crespo

Ramón contends that the American government involvement was vitally important to the success of Operation Peter Pan.

"The State Department was connected, they approved and provided the visas, and in fact let Walsh run things—he was the head of immigration for this. This circumvented normal immigration procedures. They were able to take thousands of children out of Cuba, to an unknown fate in the United States."

While the State Department handed over immigration authority to Walsh, it was the Catholic Church, on both sides, that made the program run.

"Walsh and the church officials knew it was a lie, that the Cuban government had no intention of taking over parental authority. But they took it upon themselves to convince parents their children would be better off alone in another country, knowing there was a good chance these families would never see each other again. It was the

Church and the organizers who usurped parental authority, not the Cuban government."

Ramón strongly discounts the claim that the program was motivated by noble intentions, unhesitatingly calling Operation Peter Pan a form of terrorism.

"Terrorism can take many forms—the most dramatic is a bomb in the hotel lobby, the explosion of an aircraft, the destruction of buildings. But terrorism can also be psychological. Operation Peter Pan was just such a program—aimed at the one thing parents hold most dear—their children. It destroyed thousands of families. So many of these children never saw their parents again. The parents had so much guilt, the children felt abandoned. Many of the children were abused, others were put in orphanages, others had nowhere to go. It was a terrible experience for many of them. It was a terrible abuse of Church authority."

He addresses the issue as to how the Cuban government could not have been aware of Operation Peter Pan.

"This was early in the revolution, there were many bombs and other terrorist acts taking place that the Cuban government had to deal with. The Bay of Pigs invasion [April 1961] occurred just five months before the false law was distributed. I think there was a level of awareness, and Fidel did speak of it once to denounce the lies, but there weren't a lot of resources available to determine how extensive it was. Once there was definitive proof of the fact this was an organized program, the government took steps to end it. What really slowed it down was the cancellation of the flights after October 1962. Remember, at the start the government didn't know Peter Pan was an organized operation."

The initial denouncement was against the false law. Once the scope of the Operation was revealed in 1965, the Cuban government took additional measures against the Church. However, the only priests who were ever expelled were those caught for their involvement in a plan to support a popular uprising, which never materialized. The intention was to implement the civil disturbance at the same time as Peter Pan was in full swing. A number of priests were forced to leave Cuba in September 1961, coinciding with the nationalization of Catholic schools.

Ramón comments on the emotional cost of Operation Peter Pan. "Can you imagine how the parents felt, there is nothing stronger than family in Cuba, to have these people send their children away, not knowing if they were safe, not knowing if they'd ever see them again. And then to find out it was all a lie, that the institution they had so much trust in—the Church—lied to them. It has done so much damage, psychologists have said the Peter Pan children have paid a high price, forced to grow up early, they were not prepared for the trauma of separation."

It has been called a massive form of child abuse. For those who still suffer, it's called their life.

MARINA OCHOA

"Come in, you're late, we only have the room for an hour, I don't know if we have time to show it all," Marina Ochoa is annoyed. She ushers everyone through a long hallway to a small screening room. Without hesitation she gestures the group to take a seat. Immediately the lights dim and for the next 45 minutes the screen shows her 1996 documentary, *The Other Side of the Glass*, focusing on a collection of women who live in the United States. They are all Peter Pans.

It is a powerful piece that examines the emotional toll Operation Peter Pan has enacted. These women, all in their 30s or 40s, tell their tales of the psychological damage they've dealt with, knowing how they came to the United States. Most have families of their own now but still find it difficult to come to terms with feelings of guilt and abandonment. Despite their recognition of what has been a better material life in America, it's obvious the women continue to suffer from having been wrenched from their families, particularly knowing that the Peter Pan program was developed and instituted under false pretenses. They are Americans, but their roots remain in Cuba. And in Cuba nothing is more important than family, and nothing is more traumatic than to have the family torn apart.

Marina Ochoa

Marina Ochoa, 63, comes from the artistic class in Cuba. She is a well respected film producer, having worked in the industry for years. These days she has gained the level of recognition that allows her to work freelance from her home while accessing the ICAIC film institute facilities in Havana.

The award winning *Other Side of the Glass* is one of her most important works. It is also one of her most personal through her direct connection to Peter Pan. Her brother Frank left Cuba in 1963 when he was ten years old. When he left she had no idea they'd never see each other again.

Once the showing of the documentary is complete, the conversation begins. Marina asserts herself immediately, speaking on the subject of psychological terrorism in the context of Peter Pan. She speaks passionately, mixing political perspective with social insight, combined with humor and the ironic realization as how some old black and white photos convinced her America was not the place she wanted to live.

"I was going over the concept of terrorism and I definitely do think that this episode in the history of the revolution fits perfectly with that definition. It is the consequence of the manipulation of normal fears among the Cuban bourgeois families which, up to the moment of the Triumph of the Revolution, had been the fundamental cell of Cuban society and which started to drastically lose every single element that defined it.

"The bourgeoisie was economically attacked and also attacked in its idiosyncrasy. In the economical aspect it was because of all the interventions of business, trade centers, and in its idiosyncrasy because the private schools were interfered with, they did not have the total control as before. In addition, their children started to feel independent, to make their own decisions, such as to join some of the various programs of the youth organizations, and this was appalling for the bourgeois families.

"None of this fit into their way of thinking. I lived this experience at home. I had another brother who ran away from home when he was eleven years old to go to work in the Literacy Campaign [the program to teach farmers to read and write] because my parents would not let him do so. It was a tragedy for the family. But, this was really happening. These families were in a permanent state of shock and this was manipulated. How was it manipulated? I think that the CIA, and whatever other organizations were taking part in this, including of course the Church, did not design this Operation Peter Pan, but they overlapped it with something that was naturally happening.

"There was a school here, the Ruston Academy, whose director was an American; James Baker. This school was attended by the children of important figures of Cuban society, well-to-do people. These persons were against this new revolution that was changing everything, so they asked this director to take their children out of the country so that they could be freer to act against the revolution. So, James Baker flies to Miami to meet with officials, and eventually connects with Father Bryan Walsh. Walsh was a priest who had a similar experience before with children brought from Hungary. So he knew how to deal with this type of operation.

"Baker had planned for 200 children from the Ruston school to leave, but once Walsh joins the operation, the United States government also gets involved when Walsh talks with political figures from the State Department. It was then, in my modest opinion, that the United States government overlaps the operation, taking advantage of the situation that was going on in Cuba. So a natural event is connected by an evil plotted operation. Parallel to this, a number of unscrupulous counter-revolutionary organizations start to spread their propaganda and circulate an Act of Parental Authority that they claimed to have obtained surreptitiously from the President's office.

"One has to understand the context in which this happens; a certain type of Cuban family is in shock because it is losing its influence over its children, and it is seeing how all their world is changing. So, it feels very vulnerable and full of fear. When these families see this 'law' written and, sounding like an official document that is claimed to have been obtained from the President's office, they thought it was authentic because it really looked so. This happens at a time when many new institutions had been created by the revolution like the *círculos infantiles* [day care nurseries] to contribute to the women's incorporation to jobs.

"This is how the propaganda worked, it was designed in several types; a refined one would go to the well-to-do, cultured families. But there was a type of propaganda that was addressed to the illiterate sector saying that their children would be taken to these camps in the socialist countries to later be transferred to the Soviet Union in order to make sausages out of them. And there was such a level of ignorance among some people that they believed this. This propaganda was previously preceded by an offensive waged in Latin America against Communism and the socialist countries by many publications like *Life* magazine, the *Reader's Digest*, and others. The people were ready to believe anything about the Soviet Union and the socialist countries. One can imagine this family in a shock condition hearing all these things, they decided then to take them out of Cuba to the United States.

"In 1965, five years later, the Cuban government becomes aware of this operation when they catch Ramón Grau and Pola Grau for being involved in a plot to assassinate Fidel. And 'Mongo' [Ramón] Grau, who was a despicable and cowardly individual, started to speak out all he knew and in particular about Peter Pan as an organized operation. It is then that a Migratory Act was passed by the Cuban government in which regulations are established as to children traveling alone. From then on, a child could travel alone only if, at least, one of the parents is on the other side waiting for him. That was the intent, but it didn't always work out that way.

"Although Peter Pan is not considered an act of terrorism within the traditional concept, which includes bombing, destroyed buildings, I will tell you an anecdote that illustrates that Peter Pan is something more than just a simple act of terrorism. While making the film, I interviewed a person who had been the leader of a counter-revolutionary organization ready to do any kind of terrorist act. He was shown a copy of this famous Act of Parental Authority and he asks the one who brought this copy to him if it was authentic. When the other guy said that it was not but they were going to use it for destabilization, he refuses to be part of that plot.

"So the definition of terrorism—acts of violence against civilian targets in the attempt to achieve political aims. Actions that are designed to instill fear in the general population and disrupt government functions. They can be conducted by foreigners, nationals, or exiles—well, it matches perfectly with Operation Peter Pan. There is the instillation of fear, the targets are civilian, there is a purpose to disrupt government functions, and the act is designed to achieve political aims. What else do we need to call it an act of terrorism?

"Fear was the main character; the creation of psychological and emotional conditions to manipulate a huge mass of the population in order to obtain a certain type of behavior that has a bearing, in a certain way, in a process. This is the most effective, sophisticated, and cruelest type of terrorism.

"You only have to look at the women in the film; they are all successful women in their own professional fields but that event left a permanent, devastating effect on their lives and on their emotional and spiritual nature.

"And we did not present in the film the most extreme cases, such as boys who had been raped in the camps by the priests who were in charge. We did not want to manipulate these facts or not even look like we were doing that."

Marina switches the topic to her own personal connection with Peter Pan. "My brother, Frank, my parents and I were not able to see him again. We both had the waiver visa but I had run away from home for childish reasons. After he left I felt remorse for not going with him because he was so small. I felt doubt if I was doing the right thing letting him go alone. He died in 1993 and after he left we only saw him in pictures. I went to the States in 1994, I didn't go before, because before that, communications between both countries were very restricted.

"Now, going back to the reasons why I did not want to leave Cuba; my father was a judge at the Criminal Court and used to travel a lot to the United States. Before the revolution. He greatly admired their system. You have to consider that in the 1950s only people with a high political level could realize what imperialism meant. My father was not that type of person. He considered it an ideal society. He used to go to attend conferences, meetings, and brought a lot of pictures. He loved to get his picture taken before the monuments, Lincoln, Washington, and the others. So, the image I had of the States was through these black and white pictures of people standing before something as cold as a monument and wrapped in thick coats, scarves, and a lot of snow. So, no way I would want to go there. I was 17."

Marina speaks of how the program played deviously upon the nature of its victims. "The Cuban mother is very overprotective. So you can imagine the level of terror that dominated them to get to such an extent that they sent their children out of the country alone. Many parents tried to give their babies, only a few months old, to the airhostesses to take them to the States.

"People who did not have children almost did not know about this. Perhaps someone who had a cousin did know something. But for a family that gets separated from its children you can imagine the impact. One has to remember that soon after this, relations between both countries were broken, the blockade started. It becomes more difficult to travel to the States because you had to do it through a third country and only families with money could do it. On the other hand, the propaganda of the operation was designed to tell the parents that the revolutionary government would fall soon, so they only had to wait in Cuba to bring back their children after that. The revolutionary government never fell and the breaking of the relations made it impossible for thousands of families to reunite with their children. It was a horrendous tragedy and an enormous wound in their lives.

"After many years, specifically in the '90s, many Peter Pan children came to Cuba to attend the conference 'The Nation and its Emigration' and some stated it was not their fault having been sent abroad and that they wanted to return. There are no political reasons why they haven't done so in practice. The Cuban government has no objection to this, but obviously these persons have been raised in another country with a way of life and an economic status they cannot find in Cuba and it has been difficult for them to adapt themselves to living in Cuba after so many years abroad. I know someone who came, married and lived for about four years and then left again. But that has nothing to do with the political will. It's just practical reasons. But they can come any time they want."

Marina says she has never regretted staying in Cuba. "I have all my family living there. I have had the opportunity to visit that country [the US] for months presenting my works. It's a beautiful country where there are good and intelligent people. But I feel myself bonded with my country, with its culture, and I wouldn't like to live feeling as a foreigner. I like living in my country with the rights I have, to be able to say what I want to say. It is here where my participation as an intellectual worker is appreciated and needed and where my works have an effect. And finally, and not least, my country is so beautiful."

IVETTE VEGA HERNÁNDEZ

Muchacha magazine is aimed at young Cuban girls, aged 14 to 20. Founded in 1992, it stopped publication in 1999 due to the severe paper shortage during the Special Period. It was one of many magazines that were forced to shut down during the difficult economic time of the 1990s following the collapse of the Soviet Union.

Ivette Vega Hernández

Fortunately for the female youth of the country, the go-ahead was given to resurrect the periodical in 2001. With one proviso.

"They restarted the magazine, and I was hired as the editor. But there was still no paper—I was the director of a dream. Six months later, in May 2001 the paper came, so we could start the magazine again." Ivette Vega Hernández throws back her graying hair that stylishly contours her thin face. She is a small, attractive woman with a broad, welcoming smile.

Ivette is at her office in downtown Havana on Galiano St., the prime commercial avenue of the city. The area is lined with clothing outlets, shops, restaurants and street vendors. It is where you find Havana's finest department stores, and where the famous El Encanto was firebombed in the early 1960s.

Ivette speaks fondly of her job. "The paper usually consists of 16 pages, stock paper, every three months, we distribute 100,000 copies. The goal of the magazine is to address issues for girls, but the magazine is for boys as well. There is a lot of vocational information, as teenagers that age are concerned about what they want to do with their lives. This generation, for the first time, has the opportunity to understand they don't have to see any differences between the sexes. There are no barriers for women here, the same options are available for everyone. And our goal at *Muchachas* is to promote that."

Ivette's Peter Pan connection is with her brother Julio, who has lived a troubled life. Before turning to the topic, she continues to discuss the concept of her magazine in relation to the conflicting influences of Cuban society.

"We still live in a macho culture, traditional in many respects, and there are many things that compete with the concept of the magazine, there are still problems that have to be overcome. The response to our magazine has been good, we don't get a lot of letters, people that age don't write much to magazines. But we have had many meetings with young people, very interesting gatherings where they can discuss the problems and concerns they have. That's important, and those are the issues we try to reflect in the magazine."

Ivette graduated from the University of Havana with a degree in psychology. She currently lives in the city.

"My brother Julio left Cuba as a Peter Pan, the program was basically over when he left in 1970, but there were still incidents of this happening. He was 14 years old at the time he left. I was six years old at the time. My family decided to handle the situation in a way that I wouldn't know what was happening, I guess they felt I was too young to understand. The plan was to send my brother out of the country and then the rest would leave six months later.

"He left for Madrid, Spain, with the intention to go to the United States, which he did one year later. He ended up in New York, and a few years later he moved to Miami. There's a gap in my mind as to exactly how he left. My family lived in Holguin at the time my brother was sent to Spain; my parents went to Havana after that. But they never talked about it, when this first happened I thought my brother had gone to Havana to study. I thought this even when he was in Spain. One day I just stopped seeing him, and no one talked to me to tell me what happened. I didn't see him again for 30 years."

Spain was considered to be the fourth stage of Operation Peter Pan. The Spanish Catholic Church has never determined the number of Cuban children that came through the program, although estimates range as high as 1,000. By the time Julio left the American portion of the program was for the most part over.

Both of Ivette's parents also left Cuba, "My mother left in 1991, my father left in 1994, both to be with my brother in the United States. I stayed here, alone. In 1970 when my brother left they were expecting to leave in six months, they wanted to leave to Miami, but there were restrictions."

The on-going contentious relations between the United States and Cuba have resulted in air transportation between the two countries being canceled or suspended at various times. The first incident occurred immediately following the Cuban Missile Crisis of 1962. Flights resumed a few years later, then were suspended again. Currently there is increased air traffic between Miami and Havana for Cuban-American citizens who are now permitted by the US government to travel unrestricted to the island.

It took Ivette six years after his departure before she could begin to understand what had happened to her brother.

"I was 12 when I started to comprehend what my brother was put through. In Spain he had no family there, no one. He went into the Catholic seminary. Spain was part of the Peter Pan program through the contacts in Miami. It wasn't so easy to go to Spain, but easier than getting to the United States. He went to Spain alone, I can't imagine what he went through. I didn't know anything.

"Then one day I remember I saw a letter come here. There was one person in my family who talked about that, my parents never talked about it; they kept silent about this always, especially because part of the family was against this decision. The rest of the family stayed here, no one could travel after him, so my brother felt abandoned, he felt he was told a lie. My parents told him they'd be with him in six months, and that didn't happen, so he felt discarded. It took years for them to reunite."

The separation caused tremendous emotional stress between Ivette and her parents. "They were feeling guilty. When I was twelve I applied to go to a vocational school in Havana, and around that time my parents spoke of leaving Cuba, and taking me with them. I rejected that, there were some big arguments when I knew what their plans were. I had my friends, I didn't want to leave. But they would ask me, 'Don't you want to see your brother?' I was very confused, of course I wanted to see my brother, but I didn't want to leave Cuba. And for someone at that age it's hard to deal with those feelings, that conflict."

She remembers it was in the early 1980s when, "My mother received a letter from my brother, it was the first time in years. He was very mad. That started a correspondence between my brother and my parents, this was around 1982. I was aware of this correspondence, I felt very mixed, contradictory. He was my brother, and my parents wanted to leave Cuba. I was in the middle, having to deal with these emotions, this tearing of the family."

Ivette turns to describing the psychological toll she believes the separation took on her brother.

"He never married. He had a gay affair when he came to Cuba for the first time. Now he is very ill, an alcoholic, it's been very hard for him. He's got a lot of problems. It's very difficult to be away from the land you were born in. He felt he was abandoned, with no one to go to speak to. I'm sure he felt unwanted.

"When he came to Cuba he spoke like an American, and he tried to explain things he had gone through. We understood to a certain level but he believed in another point of view regarding Cuba, he didn't know the country he was born in, so he believed so much of what was being said against Cuba. Living in the United States, by this time he was in Miami, you get that one point of view in what was going on in Cuba. In Miami most of the news about Cuba is negative. But he came to Cuba and saw things as they really are, and was able to start thinking differently, to realize the propaganda that was being told against Cuba."

Eventually, Ivette's parents were able to travel to the United States on a visitor's visa, in 1991. It was then, she said, the decision was made for the mother to stay. Half-way through this portion of the interview the emotions overcome her, she wipes away the tears while talking in a halting, low voice.

"When they were in the United States visiting my brother, my mother stayed. My father came back to Cuba, and then three years later he went. Before they went they talked to me about sharing their love, that one parent would stay in the United States with my brother, and one would stay in Cuba with me. But I said no, they have to stay together, my parents have to stay together. I was an adult by this time and could talk to them on that level. When my father came back from the United States I told him he had to return to America to be with my mother. It was a difficult, emotional time, my parents felt so guilty, they wanted to be with my brother, and with me. I wanted them to be together. Everyone was sad, but I felt it was most important for them to be together, which they are now. I think there are still a lot of issues between my brother and my parents. My brother was never able to get over the anger of being abandoned, you always need the love and care of your family, and to be sent away under those conditions, without understanding why, it was terrible."

The struggle with these emotional issues was made worse by the efforts to survive day-to-day life during the economic hardships of the Special Period. "I was always looking for things for me and my child, we suffered much during that time, things were so tough. I would receive a little sandwich daily at work, I would never eat it but take it home for my son to have. Everyone had to do things to survive, things they wouldn't normally do, like dealing with the black market.

"Every day I wondered what life would be like if I had my parents and brother living here with me. Rationally it's fair to have them with my brother, he needs them, but emotionally they are my parents as well, and I miss them, I want them with me."

Ivette breathes deeply and takes control of her emotions. She quickly returns to her normal vibrant self, recalling with a smile the second time her brother visited Cuba.

"In 1992 my brother came back, it was funny, he came loaded with so many things, he wanted us to have everything. This was during the Special Period. He met his nephew for the first time. It was funny, we were living in Havana, and at that time there were long hours of blackouts, all of a sudden we couldn't find my brother or my son, they were both named Julio. I cried out and my neighbor said my brother called a taxi—but where did they go? I didn't know he took my son. It was two or three hours later my brother called this neighbor, she had the phone, I didn't have one, and he asked if the lights had come back on. We told him yes, so he took a taxi back to the house. They had gone to the Havana Libre hotel, where they ate and drank, and my son came back with a big belly."

A year later her brother returned and Ivette took him to their hometown of Holguin. It was not as pleasant a memory.

"Things were difficult for him by then; I would never go back there again, it was too sad. He talked a lot to the neighbors, and I knew he was an alcoholic. He drank cheap rum—Chispa de Tren.

"My brother has been in the hospital, for his alcoholism, and my mother is at her limits of her strength. She has done her best, you always think love is enough to change a person, to make things right. He improves sometimes, but then falls back. My father is calm, he is more optimistic. He listens to baseball games in Cuba, on the radio in Miami, it's a way to protect himself emotionally."

She agrees that her life experiences may have had an impact on her career choice and desire to help young people navigate their way through social issues.

"What I'm doing now, I think had an influence on what I've been going through with my life. In 1997 I worked for the Cuban Women's Federation, then I applied to run the magazine. Every day I think I'm too old to run a magazine for young women, but I continue on. I realize this is a much more intelligent generation, it is sad they have been met with only difficult economic times since the 1990s. I'm optimistic about this generation, for the future of Cuba. This is not the state of socialism we believed we could build—that's due to the embargo, the energy we've had to expend to deal with the embargo, the aggression, the acts of terrorism. It has taken our focus away from the social aspects, the ability to improve things.

"I think it's important for our generation to listen to the younger generation and what they can bring to the future of Cuba. For me it would be a dream to see the improvement of relations between the United States and Cuba, for my son it's an obligation to pursue."

JUAN ESTEBAN CORTIZAS MARRERO

Juan Esteban Cortizas Marrero had his papers, visa and flight ticket to Miami. What he didn't have was control over the crisis that brought the world to the edge of nuclear war.

Juan was ten years old when he was about to become a Peter Pan. His mother and father were convinced the Cuban government was going to usurp their parental control, so the decision was made to send their young son to the United States. Everything was set. Except for the timing. The October missile crisis of 1962 intervened to put an end to those plans; as following the near nuclear disaster the American government ended all flights to and from Cuba. The decision effectively finished the American part of the Peter Pan exodus. In retrospect, Juan Esteban says, it turned out to be a fortuitous circumstance.

Juan Esteban Cortizas Marrero

"I had my passport, as well as the permit so that I could leave Cuba. This document that both parents signed was a new regulation the Cuban government instituted—you needed the written permission of both parents to leave. The Cuban government was beginning to become suspicious of what was happening to all these young children leaving Cuba. They weren't aware of the Peter Pan program yet, but they wanted to institute a system to ensure both parents were aware and agreed to send their child out of the country."

Juan Esteban, now 57 and living in Havana, is a temperate, soft-spoken man with a thick Groucho Marx moustache and wide glasses that accentuate his dark brown eyes. He admits he has never discussed this part of his life before in any official capacity. "I'm a little nervous, these are things I haven't thought of in many years. It's hard to relive this."

He has brought a slew of documents, photos and newspaper articles that outline the time in his life when he was about to leave Cuba. He shows them in a jumble of papers spread out over a large wooden table.

"I have a letter from Bryan Walsh, on February 22, 1962, from the Miami Catholic Welfare Bureau. I had been issued a visa waiver by the United States State Department on request of the Catholic Church, through Mr. Walsh's organization. I also had the letter of confirmation from Pan Am airline that my ticket and seat were ready. This is how all the Peter Pans left Cuba. I was going to be one of them."

He says he retains distinct memories of those days just before he was scheduled to leave Cuba.

"November 3, 1962, it was my father's birthday. The October crisis was October 22. I remember very well hearing about that crisis, all the flights were canceled between the United States and Cuba afterwards.

"I had my suitcase and everything else and was ready to leave. I talked a lot with my mother, I remember saying, 'No, No, I don't want to leave.' I didn't want to go to the United States alone, I had no idea what would happen to me. It was terrifying for a child at that age. I couldn't understand why my mother wanted to send me away. You think you've done something wrong, it was hard for a child that age to understand. I thought my mother didn't love me anymore, she didn't want me anymore."

He pauses momentarily and admits he continues to have a complex and painful relationship with his mother. He shows a picture of her when she was in her 30s. She is the traditional dark-haired Cuban beauty, her hair styled in the classic 1950s up-do fashion, the flowered white dress indicating the trappings of a middle class background. She left Cuba more than 30 years ago.

"My mother has been back here two times, in 1979 she was here. Her name is Orlanda, she is 81 years old and lives in the United States. I prefer she comes here to visit me. The first time my mother returned to visit in Havana, we were scheduled to meet at the Havana Libre, no wait... it was at the Havana Riviera hotel. She came into the hotel and didn't recognize me—so she came up to me and asked if I worked here at the hotel. I told her 'No, I'm your son.' I told my mother now is your chance to meet your grandchild, and they became very close.

"The second time she came, in 1996, to meet her grandson, she was here for about five days, and I worked most of the time so I didn't have much time to meet with her. I refused my mother's assistance, money, anything. I refused her offers of money, I didn't want it. I have latent hostility towards my mother, she tried to send me away, when I was just a child, I could never understand that. Maybe she wanted to make it up to me someway offering me money, but I wanted to have the peace of mind to reject it.

"I was angry with my mother, very angry with what she tried to do. And I wasn't sent away, so I can imagine that anyone who is an actual Peter Pan would be angry, to be sent to a different country, without anyone you knew to meet you on the other side. To be taken by the Church, put in homes, in foster homes, so many suffered abuse, the mental difficulties. It was a horrible plan and so many parents let their children go, never to see them again."

Juan is now married with a daughter, Izzet, 35 and a son, Javier, who is 19 years old and studying at the University of Havana.

The obvious question elicits a firm and immediate response. "I have no regret not going to the United States. Despite all the difficulties we face here, I have no regrets. I remember all that they have done to the victims in Cuba, all the terrorist acts they have committed. This history of Cuba you can not hide, because there are so many people who have died, you can't forget that. It may not be well known, but you can't hide the facts. I'm happy to have stayed here. My grandparents were born in Spain, and there is a new law in Spain that all people born in Cuba can get a Spanish passport. But I have no intention, I have no desire to leave Cuba."

NOEL BETANCOURT

Noel Betancourt lives on the sixth floor of a narrow apartment building in Vedado, downtown Havana. He is thin, above average height and wears wide black glasses that give a professorial appearance. His balding hair adds to the impression of an academic background.

His story is unique. A Cuban teenager from a successful business-class family during the Batista era; he left as a test case of the Peter Pan process at the age of 18, only to return to his country more than 30 years later. His English is excellent, his Spanish impeccable and he brings a unique perspective to the controversial Peter Pan program.

Noel Betancourt

The experience has left a psychological mark as he has struggled throughout the majority of his 65 years with who he is and where he belongs. He's searched for an identity throughout his transient life, in Cuba during the early years, in the United States, Europe, Latin America, then back to his homeland. He says his life experiences have led him through a personal, social and political awaking that has returned him to "my fatherland." His is a story of the search for self awareness and acceptance for his belief in the social aspect of man.

Noel is also dissimilar in regards to the Peter Pan connection. Technically he doesn't match the profile of the program. Some consider him to have been too old—the program was aimed primarily at young Cuban children, not teenagers. For another, the timing was a little off, he left Cuba in October 1960; the Peter Pan operation is generally accepted to have begun in December 1960. But he is a Peter Pan, one of the first test cases that proved the program worked. He, along with his brother and sister left Cuba under the format and visas that church officials in Miami, with the support of their Cuban Catholic counterparts, would utilize to bring out an estimated 14,000 children over the next two years. Noel came out on the I-20 visa, and once American and Cuban church officials realized how easy it was to obtain, the plan was put in to place to convince Cuban families to send their children to America, alone, in order to prevent the communist government from assuming parental authority.

Noel welcomes his guests and comments on the long climb up from the street to reach his apartment. Immediately he speaks of his obsession.

"I run four kilometers a day, I've been doing it for six years. It was like a revelation for me, once I started running, a little at first, then more and more every time until I got up to four kilometers, there was an incredible change in how I was feeling. I have so much more energy, physically and mentally, and I sleep better, eat better, just feel better. It's like a smoker who quits then compares his health to when he was smoking to when he quit. I run every morning, rain or shine."

His running, he says, afforded him a physical revelation. His life story has brought him to an important intellectual truth.

"Peter Pan, well yes and no. I and my brothers left Cuba before Peter Pan officially started. But the way we left Cuba was directly related to how Peter Pan operated, without doubt. Maybe we were the test cases."

He speaks rapidly of the influence the Catholic Church held over certain segments of Cuban society before and after the revolution.

"American intention was married to the Catholic Church in Cuba, together they made Peter Pan. My family was close to the Catholic Church, I was a member of the middle class, and the church was very important in Cuba at that time. Before the revolution the church was a rich people's church, the Catholic Church almost didn't exist in the lower classes or in the countryside. The Protestant Church had more impact on the poor, they were more involved in social programs. The Catholic Church was more influential with the upper classes and those who lived in the cities.

"The Catholic Church was an important institution before, remember, they had a social function for all of us. The pastors would guide political activities, and have influence with the children when they felt it was appropriate. The political belief at that time for my social class, which was the upper class, was homogeneous. Cuba was very different from any other country in that respect. There were great splits between the classes, and the upper classes controlled the economy, and directed the politics of the country, under American guidance."

Throughout the interview Noel shows himself to be a very exacting speaker. The slightest variation from the point he wants to make is immediately corrected, and he expresses himself intensely and confidently. His arms are constantly in motion in support of his conversational points.

"After the revolution the upper class went to Miami to wait it out. There was no doubt in their minds that this would pass in a few weeks, and things would get back to normal. That's why they left, they were absolutely convinced the Americans would invade and they figured there would be a lot of blood. They didn't want to be here for that. They were scared shitless when the socialists marched. So you can see it from their side, from Miami. And they are still waiting in Miami. They are still waiting for the revolution to pass, all these years they are still waiting.

"Fidel was an attractive figure for me, I was very nationalistic. At first he wanted to merge the middle class with national business priorities, including changes to land ownership, distribution and capital. By 1960 everyone knew that was just a lost dream. There were both internal and external reasons for that, remember how the United States government reacted to the revolution, very negatively, well before Cuba moved towards communism. But the revolution was turning communist and my father knew he'd lose his business. When the bosses left, when those who owned businesses left Cuba, the government took over. But my father held on to the last minute. He was worried to see that the children left before him, to make sure we were safe.

"I was 18, my brother Héctor was 17, my sister Carmen was twelve and my youngest brother Rafael was seven. My father wanted us all to leave. Rafael was too young to be sent, it was decided, so he was going to leave with my parents.

"Other Cuban children were being sent away, the key was to get a visa. And it was the Church that started to facilitate the exit visas, which was the essence of Peter Pan. It was the development of a system that obtained exit visas for students first, then for children. The University of Miami was involved at the first stages. I was registered to attend the University as a condition for getting the visa. With this proof you could get the I-20 visa and go to the United States. The relationship with the University was only to arrange the visa, and when the Church realized this was possible they started to take over the program. We were the test cases for Peter Pan—and it worked perfectly. No, I never set foot at the University of Miami.

"We were one of the first children to leave Cuba, when the Church found out about how easy it was to get this visa then everything moved quicker. Once this was established there were a number of people who helped things along. It's so hard to imagine how a parent could send his child away, but those were difficult times and the Church took advantage.

"Church officials even went so far as to knock on the doors of Cuban parents, convincing them to fill out documents to allow their children to leave Cuba under these I-20 visas. They created so much fear in these people that they would willingly give up their children. It was incredible. And terrible, such an abuse of power. It was terrorism."

Noel remembers those difficult first days in America. "I had an uncle who lived in Miami, he was working as a bank official. He promised my father that he'd receive us, but only for a few weeks. He couldn't afford to feed us all for longer than that. We then went to New York City. When we got there, I remember it was snowing. It was the first time I had seen a snowfall.

"My sister, her connection with the church was better. She lived in a nun community. They had a house in Pennsylvania, 50 miles from Philadelphia. They had a school there and they took her in. She and my other brother still live in the United States, my younger brother lives here, he returned as well. No, I don't keep in contact with the two who live in America.

"My father was very worried about us, it was only my brother and myself who went to New York. My father had contacted the Church in Cuba in regards to where I would stay in the United States. My father went to speak to the Jesuits, and they had many foreign contacts. One was Fordham University in New York. It was very hard to get the Jesuits to aid us, but one priest, he said yes, send them to us at Fordham. The director got pissed off when he found out about this arrangement; he said there was no place to put us. But we had already arrived, there was this big snowstorm going on outside, and there was nowhere else to go. So we slept in the infirmary, we cried all that first night.

"We were scared, hungry, and didn't have any idea what we would do. We couldn't stay there, we had no money, nowhere else to go, but they wouldn't let us stay there. This was one Catholic link that didn't work out. But there were many other incidents where the Catholic Church immediately opened their doors. And when Peter Pan got underway it was all set up beforehand, so situations like ours wouldn't occur. So again I guess we were test cases, we showed that sending children out of Cuba was one thing, but there had to be arrangements confirmed on the other side. Unfortunately, even with these arrangements there were terrible things, children sent to foster homes, beaten and abused, children separated, living horrible lives."

Noel stayed in New York for nine months, returning after to Miami. "I was doing nothing in New York. It was a terrible winter. By that time my parents had left Cuba, to Miami, so I went to live with my parents. I was 19 or 20 when I moved back in with my parents in Miami. I wanted to go to university. I had a friend in Louisville who said I should go there, so I went and got my degree. Later I got a good job in Philadelphia. I lived there for four years. I got married to an American girl and we decided to go to Europe, this was around 1967."

After a year in Europe Noel returned to the United States and began connecting with his Cuban identity.

"When we went back to the United States I became politically aware. It was the time of the Vietnam War, the civil rights movements, social awakenings. I started to look towards Cuba at a different light, more sympathetic. I started to realize I had lived a social revolution in Cuba, so I started to look more into politics.

"I lived the war against Batista and Fidel's Revolution. It was back in my mind and I started to use it, now with a different kind of perspective. I was in conflict with my parents, who held the opposite view of the revolution and social aspects. I started reading social subjects, and this helped further politicize my thinking, and I started to realize maybe these people are right what they are doing in Cuba, I was having a different outlook on life, the future was becoming different.

"I changed the roots of the terms of the way of life, I was making commitments in a different direction. The strongest commitment was to national identity, I stopped trying to be an American. I was tired of the option of being a second class family member in my wife's family. So I said to her, 'come to Cuba with me or stay here.' Latin America was the second choice, if it wasn't Cuba then it'd be Latin America, so we went to Puerto Rico and got involved with certain groups who were in the struggle for their independence. I lived in San Juan for three years, the links there got colder, the movement quieted. Then I got a job in Caracas, Venezuela, and stayed there for five years."

At that time Noel remembers that things were changing somewhat in regards to immigration policy in Cuba. "This was, 1979 or 1980. So there was more interest on my part to explore the possibility of returning."

He was also developing a new attitude towards the anti-Castro community in Miami.

"I was finding that other Cubans my age were going through similar processes, there were different characteristics but one common element—that was a sympathy for Cuba, and the rejection of the hard-line Cuban community in Miami.

"There was an expression, I don't think it's much used these days. We started calling the hard line anti-revolutionaries *Souewsera*—it is an invented term loosely describing the area where the first Cubans settled in Miami after the revolution. They settled in the South West quadrant of Miami. It was an extremely derogatory word to describe the lifestyle, not the politics, but the lifestyle of these people—it was the Mafia, the dirty lifestyle, an obnoxious lifestyle that represented the corruption and control during Batista's day. There is no real spelling for this word, you won't find it in the dictionary.

"I returned to Cuba in 1980. It was a simple but truthful decision. It was like a revelation. Like my running. It was like a lightning bolt that struck me. Of course there were many things going on with me to bring me to that direction. Vietnam for one thing. There were a lot of changes in me, much turmoil. There were so many identity problems I was going through. At the time I was reading so much Cuban literature. I became affected by the ideas of Fidel, which played an important part. And just the constant questioning of yourself. My age was a factor, I left Cuba when I was 18 years old so many of my formative years were spent in Cuba. I had seen the Batista regime personally, and understood the terrible things it was doing to the country. And then I saw the new ideas under Fidel, but was sent away so soon after that. I've been back for 27 years. I was an unusual case; to come back to Cuba was not something normal.

"Cuba was exactly what I thought it would be when I came back. When I came here it was pretty much as I thought it would feel—this is the politics I wanted. This is my revolution. All else became secondary. The material things were here for me, for what I wanted. The important things were not material, it was the social aspects of the Cuban Revolution that were important."

Once in Cuba, Noel had to deal with a new reality. "I am an electrical engineer, I had no problem to find a job, but there were things I did find hard to adjust to. My neighbors accepted me, once they knew who I was and what I was for, there was no problem. Personal things, everyone wants things to improve. But everyone makes choices. I had an air conditioner here in my apartment. I don't turn it on anymore because it's too expensive, the electrical rates went up. And so I decided not to use the air conditioner anymore. I have a car, I decided to keep the car. I'd rather drive than use the air conditioning, so that's my choice. And everyone makes choices, no matter what system you live under."

His return to Cuba, however, did not solve his ongoing identity crisis.

"I've had a problem with identity all my life. I wasn't a typical person of my social class when in Cuba. The rich only cared about themselves, and there was such a huge gap between the small amount of rich and the vast majority of the poor. When Fidel came I identified with so many of his ideas, where the most of the upper classes were horrified. Then I moved to America and I didn't feel I was American. So I wasn't Cuban in Cuba, or American in the United States. It led me to a period of being anti-social, I didn't like people."

And now? Noel smiles and admits, "I am extremely happy to be back in Cuba, the politics, the sense of community here. I love Cuba, love my country. It fills me. I have no regrets. I have everything I want here. You ask about the criticism of the system here, the things the United States government points to as restrictions. Those are not important to me or to many Cubans. What is important is the sense of community support, to working towards something for the good of all, not just for the individual."

He pauses momentarily, struggling to find the exact word in English. Waving his hand and rising from the couch, Noel moves quickly to the bedroom. A few seconds pass before he returns, a dictionary in hand. Rapidly the pages flip by. He stops and smiles.

"The legitimacy, that's the word, the legitimacy of the Cuban Revolution. I found that out to be true soon in this process of my coming back to Cuba. The more I grew the more I grew into it. The more I saw the revolution the more I see the legitimacy. I'm proud of it. And this is something the Cuban-Americans who are against the revolution will never understand. The legitimacy it has.

"All this has helped me to develop a social political sense. I see people here in Cuba not supporting the revolution, and they want to go back to before. You are stupid, you are an asshole. That's what I want to tell them. There are many ways to improve things here, of course, but it is so stupid to think to go back to the way they were before the revolution. I lived both sides, I saw what it was like before, I lived that lifestyle. I lived 20 years of the capitalist experience, when I was 20 to 40 years, the most formative time of life.

Noel ends the interview with an observation of the near future for Cuba.

"There are two options in the next five years—we might be worse than Iraq regarding a military invasion. Or this is the best moment in our history, that we have made it. I'm very optimistic, we have turned the corner. Both here and in the United States things are just beginning and I want to see what happens."

5
Biological Terrorism

Anthrax, Dengue, Botulism, Hepatitis, Influenza, Typhus, Encephalitis, Swine Fever, Avian Flu, Sugar Cane Rust, Tobacco Fungus, Potato, Rice, Corn, Cereal Pest. The list goes on.

The catalogue of biological terrorism that the Cuban government asserts has been inflicted upon the population is impressive. It is also difficult to prove it to an absolute certainty. There is, however, a substantial amount of evidence, circumstantial and otherwise, that has accrued during the past four-plus decades to point to the intentional introduction of a variety of deadly germs—evidence including documentary corroboration, testimonials, scientific expertise, eyewitness verification and even confessions. And more than 100 dead children.

According to the scientists and international health agencies who have studied these occurrences, there is little doubt that the outbreaks of deadly viruses were not natural events.

To prove it categorically, however, is where the difficulty arises. While the facts lend themselves to trends and indications, proof is based on negatives and suppositions. The experts have accumulated a body of information that points strongly to the actuality of biological terrorism, but as scientists they hesitant to speak in absolutes. What they can do is present the data and allow others to draw conclusions. Combine the scientific knowledge with known American government involvement in biological experiments, its history of aggression towards Cuba, and with the more than willing anti-revolutionary organizations in Florida—intent moves into the realm of possibility. Unfortunately, while the ends are evident, the means remains speculative.

However, in the case of this form of terrorism against Cuba, there is more than just scientific research and evidentiary indicators. There is sworn testimony from Cuban-Americans; eyewitness accounts, and even double agent intrigues.

To that end, a number of highly regarded Cuban scientists and experts were brought together to discuss the evidence, as well as to talk about barking dogs and quacking ducks.

One of the country's top experts studying the link between the various outbreaks and their intentional introduction is Ariel Alonso Pérez, author and historian.

"There have been a minimum 23 events of biological terrorism against Cuba where there is extensive evidence that shows these viruses and agents were introduced into the country. There are common elements and that helped me identify universal characteristics. What are the characteristics? The main one is the appearance of these biological agents not in a natural way. The symptoms show these agents appear in a more aggressive form and are populated faster. Scientifically, there is no justification for these agents to appear prior in natural form, so the logical conclusion is they had to be introduced into the country."

Ariel points to a substantial amount of data on the non-scientific side of the issue.

"You have the sworn confession of Cuban-Americans saying they were hired to spray chemical agents in Cuba, to start the biological war. There are documents, newspaper reports, testimony from former CIA agents who outline the meetings that took place specifically to plan how to conduct biological terrorism against Cuba, how to introduce these organisms into our country. There is no doubt this was biological terrorism."

In January 1977 *Newsday*, followed by the *Washington Post*, *Le Monde*, the *Guardian* and others, published interviews with a former CIA agent who confessed he was part of the operation to introduce swine fever to Cuba in the early 1970s. The agent, not named but suspected to be Philip Agee, claimed the fever was introduced from the Guantánamo Naval Base at the southern end of Cuba. Evidence was also presented that at Fort Gulick in Panama, a CIA agent handed over a vial of biological micro organisms to pass on to Cuban-American groups with the intent to introduce them to Cuba.[1]

An extensive 1982 article from *Covert Action* outlined the intentional introduction of Dengue 2 to Cuba.[2] It has also been well documented that the United States government conducted various research projects into biological warfare, including Dengue fever in 1959 at Fort Derrick in Maryland, and the Walter Reed Army Institute in Washington.[3] Pentagon officials suggested a chemical and bacterial program to contaminate Cuba's food supplies, and part of the sabotage criteria under Operation Mongoose was to induce failures in food crops.[4]

Ariel's written research has uncovered numerous incidents, including the case of the cattle disease brucellosis, where a Cuban official operating a veterinarian lab in Camagüey, Alexis Casal Bravo, confessed he was working with the CIA to alter the results of tests on the cattle. Bravo told authorities he knew the disease had been introduced into Cuba. Brucellosis causes spontaneous abortion in infected animals.[5]

"There is ample evidence of biological terrorism against Cuba, and when you put it up against how the diseases were spread, how they affected the island, in my opinion there is little doubt as to what happened. Dengue 2 is a perfect example as to how this disease could not have occurred naturally," Ariel states.

In agreement is Luis Pérez Vicente, director of Exotic Disease Quarantine, Plants and Pests, who spoke of the most devastating case of biological terrorism inflicted upon Cuba.

"Hemorrhagic Dengue 2 was not found in other parts of the Caribbean when Cuba was affected by this epidemic in 1981, nor were there any cases in Cuba at the time. There is virtually no way it could have been brought into Cuba accidentally, or naturally. It appeared in Cuba in an unusual form, in three different parts of the country at the same time."

The three areas—Havana, Cienfuegos and Camagüey—lie hundreds of miles apart, although within a straight line from one side of the island to the other.

Luis Pérez continued that once Dengue hit, "There were interchanges, lectures among the experts, and we spoke to scientists from other parts of the world—there was a tremendous exchange of information. The first stages of the operational mode were to study the event, to study the spread of the disease, once it was determined it was Dengue 2, to gain information as to how the disease affected people, and how to treat it. Then we put it in context as to what happened before, aspects such as determining the CIA had special interest in these matters.

"As well, this is unrelated to Dengue, in 1982 the Cuban government knew the CIA had asked one of our double agents what information there was of any problems regarding agriculture in Cuba; and specifically talked about two biological agents. A little time after, we detected an epidemic of a bird disease in Santiago and Baracoa. It had never been in that area before. So there is a connection directly between the introduction and the event. The investigation of this bird disease was conducted by one of the most famous Cuban scientists, Oscar Viamontes Becerra, PhD biologist. He was able to isolate this virus, and he discovered that the characteristic of this variation didn't correspond to any variation in nature, so it had to be manipulated artificially. It was the worst variant of the virus, affecting all types of birds. For scientists it is hard to say it is absolute proof of intentional manipulation and introduction, but the circumstantial evidence is overwhelming—there is a pattern we can determine. This is the difficulty in all of these studies; it is impossible to say 100 percent the diseases were introduced intentionally; but when you look at the evidence, in total, it is also next to impossible not to come to that conclusion."

Carlos Delgado, sub-director of the Institute of Veterinarian Medicine in Havana, points out that the deductions one can draw from the evidence are more substantive these days, thanks to the advances in scientific technology.

"The techniques to find and understand the evidence are better now, particularly in the field of molecular verification, and this allows scientists to say in stronger terms that these diseases were introduced outside of Cuba. Dengue 2, it is 99 percent certain that it was introduced."

International agencies also studied the outbreak. In September 1981 the Pan American Health Organization (PAHO) sent American scientist Dr. Robert J. Tonn, regional advisor of medical entomology, to investigate. In his final report he wrote, "The cause of the hemorrhagic dengue disease is still unknown, despite the suggestion of some advanced theories. The sudden appearance of the disease in Cuba remains a mystery."[6]

And for those who don't believe the scientific evidence, then there is something more direct. "We have the confession of the man who said he did it," Luis states calmly.

Eduardo Arocena, a Cuban American connected to Miami-based anti-revolutionary group Omega 7, confessed in 1984 that he had visited Cuba in 1980 in connection with a mission to introduce "some germs" into the country, as reported by the *New York Times*. Arocena's testimony came during his trial in New York for his connection with the assassination of Cuban diplomat Felix Garcia in front of the United Nations building in 1980, and with other bombings in the United States against Cuban interests.[7]

At his trial he testified, "The mission of the group was to obtain certain germs to introduce them to Cuba to start the chemical war in Cuba." One of those was Dengue 2.[8]

Ariel recounts another incident in October 1996 when "A Cubana Fokker [F-27] airplane flying from Havana to Holgiun above the international air corridor observed above him a small plane with

American markings flying north. At this moment the Cuban pilot Erián Romero Liuth observed a spray of smoke coming from the American plane, which he reported to the control tower. He also contacted directly the American plane and asked if there was any problem, the pilot responded no. I have seen the report from Cubana aviation officials and the dialogue between the pilots.

"A month later the area below where the plane flew farmers reported the plague thrips palmi which affects various vegetable products. This was during the Special Period when the government was experimenting with various forms of increased food production including through agroponics."

Switching back to the scientific side; Luis Pérez compared the way that scientists look at these issues to the way a detective approaches a murder case.

"We look for circumstantial evidence, one of the factors is where the disease appears. For example rice mite, this affected the best rice farms in Cuba, only the best rice farms, so why was that? You look at when and where they hit and where they have had the most impact. Why they affected only certain areas, at certain times, when they were not appearing before or anywhere else. There are many examples of this type. Tobacco blue mold, it did not appear in Cuba until 1979. This is the most devastating type of mold against tobacco. This type of blue mold is only comparable in Australia, so our conclusion was that it had to be the source. While I don't have proof of the connection, it is completely different from any blue mold elsewhere. So how did it come to Cuba? Scientifically there is no evidence that it came to Cuba naturally; so what is the other alternative? It had to be introduced intentionally."

He concludes with the legal metaphor, "If this was a murder trial, and we brought all this circumstantial evidence, forensic, scientific evidence, an eye-witness account, and motive, I think we'd get a conviction, even if there was no weapon found."

While there may not be obvious natural explanations, there are various methods to introduce the disease intentionally.

"It is easy to bring this virus in, as a tourist, businessman, anyone can do it and it is virtually impossible to detect. Cuba once had an important banana program, now nothing. You have to understand how damaging this can be, to the people, to our economy. And that's the purpose of the biological terrorism, to cause the government to expend resources, money and energy. And to have a negative effect on the population," Luis Pérez says.

Estimates indicate it has cost the Cuban government hundreds of millions of dollars to combat the various forms of biological terrorism. A spraying program continues for the control of Dengue 2. The sugar cane rust annually destroys between 15 to 20 percent of the crop, and an estimated $400 million in worldwide sales was lost when the tobacco mold hit.

Lydia Margarita Tablada Romero is general director of the National Center for Animal and Plant Health, in San José. She comments further on the swine fever and the impact it had.

"The first outbreak of swine fever was 1971, the western provinces were affected initially, south of Havana. When the revolution first triumphed, there were no plans to develop these biological attacks against Cuba, it was only after the revolution devoted itself to guarantee food to the people that these attacks started to develop. The swine fever was devastating, the first sick animals were destroyed rapidly, but then so many more started to die. We brought specialists from abroad to help make the diagnosis. In one month the fever spread and we had to kill all the stock of pigs. We had to sacrifice 500,000 pigs, it took years to recover."

Lydia continues, outlining the investigation that was conducted when Cuban cattle started to get sick, again in 1981. That year was known as the year of the plague as African swine flu, tobacco blue mold, sugar cane rust, Dengue 2, influenza, meningitis and hemorrhagic conjunctivitis all hit Cuba within a span of a few months.

"The cattle in Villa Clara, in the central province, were affected first. We didn't destroy the cattle, we were able to treat them, at great expense. We brought in experts to investigate, because it hit so suddenly. The disease was spread through contact. One French scientist came and he had no explanation as to how it was started, it was determined that it was not possible to have this occur naturally. It had never been in Cuba before, but now it was spreading throughout the country. This caused serious economic problems. We tried to import the chemicals and insecticides to combat this, but it was difficult to do because of the blockade."

Lydia comments that there are now substantial resources dedicated to combat the continuing biological warfare against the country.

"Under the central plant quarantine program there are 15 provincial labs, 67 plant protection stations, 2,250 professionals working. There is a huge amount of infrastructure and resources dedicated to this. With these new technologies we can determine better if the diseases are similar to other varieties, which gives us more evidence whether it is naturally occurring or intentionally manipulated."

While professional ethics would prevent her from signing a sworn avadavat stating unequivocally that these diseases were brought into Cuba, she allows herself to recite an axiom that expresses succinctly her point of view: "Si camina como un perro, ladra como un perro, y tiene rabo de perro… es un perro'—which translates: If it runs like a dog, barks like a dog, and has a tail like a dog… it's a dog. The English version simply changes the dog into a duck: If it looks like a duck, walks like a duck, quacks like a duck… it's a duck.

Cuba's efforts to bring these biological terrorism attacks to the attention of the international community have included protests to the United Nations. To mixed results, Lydia admits.

"In the United Nations we spoke of all the biological terrorism directed against Cuba. Some scientists have supported us, especially the ones who have seen all the evidence, and those who have come here as well. But again, it is so hard to come up with absolute irrefutable evidence. Even with the sworn confessions of these pilots, people don't believe us. But the work we and others have done all points to the facts that these diseases were not naturally occurring. You then look at the blockade, the other acts of terrorism that have been committed against our country, the evidence the United States has been involved in biological work. All this points in one direction. But you have to decide yourself. They discovered in bean crops, during the Special Period, these pests that didn't exist in Cuba previously. How is this possible? It's easy to send a plane from Florida over to Cuba, to spray, it's easy to do this. And there is solid evidence that this has happened before, many times. We've had eyewitnesses say they have seen these planes with spray coming out of them, planes that are not Cuban, they should not be in the area. This is very serious for us—this isn't just affecting plants or animals, but it is killing people as well."

DENGUE FEVER

In a matter of less than six months, from June to October 1981, more than 300,000 Cubans across every part of the country were stricken by hemorrhagic Dengue 2—the deadliest form of the disease. The initial outbreak appeared on the island simultaneously in three different areas. At its worst, 68,000 cases were treated in the one-week period from June 30 to July 6. Before the epidemic was brought under control 158 people died, of which 101 were children under the age of 14.

Since those months in 1981 the Cuban government has been forced into an annual spraying campaign to control the Dengue carrying Aedes mosquito, the same one that transmits yellow fever. Estimated cost to the Cuban government to date—$100 million—a higher than expected cost due to the blockade.

The symptoms of Dengue 2 include fever, watery eyes, runny nose, headache, back ache, insomnia, lack of appetite and extreme bone pain. Internal bleeding and shock follows. It is particularly virulent in the bodies of young children.

The Aedes mosquitoes bite during the day, achieving maximum effect in high density urban areas. The disease moves rapidly. Scientists have shown it is relatively easy to spread mosquitoes from planes or boats, miles away from the Cuban shorelines, and have the insects reach land with little difficulty on the air currents.

Which is exactly what experts suspect happened in 1981 when cases were discovered in three different areas—Havana, Cienfuegos and Camagüey. While hundreds of miles apart, the three locations lie within a straight line from one side of the island to the other.

The initial cases were examined extensively by the Cuban Ministry of Public Heath. It was determined that none of the original victims had traveled out of the country or had contact with foreigners. At the time of the outbreak Cuban officials also examined all visitors who had arrived from known Dengue areas—Vietnam, Laos, Africa. The examinations showed the disease was not introduced by an infected visitor.

The fact Dengue spread at such an astonishing rate led Cuban officials and scientists to offer no other reasonable explanation but the artificial introduction of mosquitoes. To make sure, however, assessments were conducted to see if there were other outbreaks occurring in neighboring Caribbean islands.

While Cuba suffered more than 300,000 cases of hemorrhagic Dengue within six months, no cases were being reported in either Jamaica or Bahamas, two of the closest islands to the areas where the disease had struck in Cuba. In all of the Caribbean only 6,000 cases of Dengue were reported during this time—but only in Cuba were the cases hemorrhagic. Confirmation of this came from the Pan American Health Organization. The Cuban Ministry of Public Health, supported by other international health organizations and independent scientists, concurred.[9]

ANA ELBA CAMINERO

She is a short, thickset woman, with close-cut black hair and deep brown eyes. Her face betrays the mother's pain she has carried for the past 30 years. She looks tired, sad and older than her 64 years.

Ana Elba Caminero

Ana Elba's story revolves around her two daughters, one who survived, one who did not.

"My younger daughter, Janet Chacón, was six-and-a-half when she died. My older daughter Isnavis Chacón was twelve years old when she became sick, at the same time. She lived, and is now 39 years old. It was June, 1981 when Janet died."

Ana Elba's daughters were among the first cases of hemorrhagic Dengue 2. Before the disease was brought under control more than 100 children and dozens of adults lost their lives.

"I was the first one who became sick, the disease has different appearances, the three of us had different symptoms, but we were all affected. I had red spots on my arms, lot of fever, pain all over my body, with a lot of pain in my head. In June I was sick almost the whole month. On June 7 my younger daughter felt bad, then the older one got sick.

"They both had pain in the stomach, fever, vomited blood. I didn't go to the hospital right away, yes I thought it was serious, but I didn't go to the doctor, I just gave myself aspirin and I did get better. I just thought it was the flu or something, no one knew what was going on at that time.

"But my children, yes, they went right to the hospital. The doctors gave them medicine to lower the fever. In the afternoon we took the youngest one to the hospital; that was on June 9. On the 10th she died, at night. I had no idea how sick she was, in the hospital she got worse and worse. The doctors didn't know what she had. I don't remember when she died if the doctors said what it was, but I don't think so because they didn't discover the disease until later. They did everything they could, all the medicine they gave her. But nothing worked. She died in a lot of pain. I remember her crying, she was scared. She didn't understand. I was with her when she died, I held her, I held her in my arms for a long time.

"My older daughter, she had menstruation already and she had it a few days before. On the 10th the older one gets a high fever. I told the doctors that already I had one younger daughter die today. I was not thinking straight, I had no time to react to my younger daughter dying, there was no time to mourn, as I had to take care of my older daughter."

Ana does her best to control her emotions, remembering how frustrated the medical staff was.

"The doctor who took care of the younger one, on the night she died he was so angry, crying, he hit the wall out of frustration, he felt so impotent that he couldn't do anything to save her life, he couldn't do anything, he didn't know what it was.

"I had to go to the funeral of the younger one, I was at the cemetery in the morning, and then I had to go to the hospital in the afternoon. I buried one while the other one was sick, and I didn't know if she was going to live or die." Ana's stoicism fails her. She cries softly while trying to continue.

"It was June 11, after burying the little one I asked the doctors, but they said they didn't know how the older one will go, but thought she might survive because she was older, stronger. You can not imagine how difficult it was for me. The older one was aware of what happened to her little sister, and she knew she had the same disease. We only had two children. I had to comfort the older one all the time she was in the hospital. It was so hard for me to encourage her, I was so afraid she would die as well.

"This lasted for seven days, then finally the older one started to respond to the medicine and the care. There were other people who wanted to take care of her, other family members and friends. But I wouldn't let them, I was with her at the hospital all the time day and night. The doctors told me there was no remedy, but they trusted that she was strong. Thankfully she did recover fully, and to this day there have been no lasting effects. But it was the worst week of my life."

Ana Elba remembers the support of friends and family, and how important it was.

"There was a lot of help from family, friends and everyone in the neighborhood. But no one other than the mother can understand this horror. I was in the washroom at the hospital after the younger one died, and I felt a huge pain in my chest, the stress of it was overcoming me. I had to be optimistic to the older one, talk to her, to tell her it's not the same as what happened to her younger sister, that she was older and stronger and would survive. I was very worried for her but I had to tell her that everything would be OK, that she wouldn't die. But I thought she would die, because no one knew what it was. It was a terrible, terrible time. I had no chance to grieve for the younger one; the hardest part was to put on a good face for my older daughter, because she still was alive. Dengue is worse in younger children, until 14 years old it is more dangerous, after that the chance of survival is good. But there are cases of adults dying from this disease.

"So the older one was close to that age of 14, and that was a big reason she survived. After a few days she was released from hospital and was at home, the doctors came over and told us it was Dengue. The time my older one was in the hospital gave the doctors time to do tests and find out what it was. I was so focused on the little one I didn't know what was happening around the older one.

"After it was found out that it was this type of Dengue, the country had a lot of problems to get the resources to control this disease, the chemicals, including interferon, it was hard to get. It's still hard to get, in part because of the embargo. I think many more lives could have been saved if not for the difficulties in getting these substances."

Ana Elba lets herself smile just a little as she relates her direct involvement in helping control the disease.

"When they spray my house I'm most attentive to what they are doing. And I'm very active in my neighborhood to make sure every house gets sprayed. There are some people who don't want their house sprayed, when I find that out I go over and talk to them, to make sure they understand how important the spraying is.

She quietly reflects on how Dengue 2 arrived to Cuba. "This is an act of terrorism that continues to this day. We did not have this disease before. An investigation showed that it was introduced. Eduardo Arocena, he was at a trial, I think in New York, for another thing, but he confessed then that he was assigned on this mission to obtain certain germs and introduce them into Cuba. He's never been tried for that crime, there was no further investigation taken by the Americans.

"You can imagine how I feel about that. This person, and all involved, they have a debt with me and with all the Cuban people. It is one of the many forms of terrorism, there have been many types of biological terrorism that have been brought to Cuba, but this Dengue is the worst because it affects the young ones."

Ana Elba ends the interview with the hope that her experience may bring a better appreciation of the effect terrorism has had on her homeland.

"I have a message to the United States government, I don't know the exact words, but my desire to express, that the entire world knows about these things against Cuba, these acts of terrorism. But the American people have to pay a little more attention to what's been happening to Cuba. It has been such a big damage, how much all these acts of terrorism have affected such a small country, such a small country that is just trying to defend itself, defend its freedom."

EDILFREDO SOSA PÉREZ

This imposing, gray-haired man has worked at hard labor all his life; it shows in the deep lines in his hands, the wrinkles in his face. Edilfredo's physical hardships, however, are secondary to the emotional scar he's lived with for the past 30 years.

Edilfredo Sosa Pérez
with daughter and
granddaughter

Edilfredo, 59, resides in the picturesque town of Colon, located 150 kilometers south-east of Havana, in Matanzas province. This hustling community is named after Christopher Columbus (Cristóbal Colón in Spanish), and history's most famous explorer is commemorated here by an imposing statue in the middle of the town square. Although it's well accepted that the man who discovered America never got anywhere near Colon, the pride in sharing some part of his fame is not diminished by that fact.

Edilfredo's story revolves around his beloved daughter Norka Sosa Coto. She was eight years old when she died, and though it happened more than three decades ago Edilfredo can't let it go, or reconcile himself over the loss.

"You never get over something like this, how can you? I remember vividly when it happened, I was working for the army in Colon; previously I was in Havana, I was divorced and living in Mariano [Havana]. My wife was living in Lawton. Then I was mobilized here in Colon in 1977 at the army camp.

"Almost every weekend I went to Havana to visit my daughter, in a bus it took about four or five hours from Colon. Back then the transportation systems were better. I remember, I was at the army camp and received a radio message that my daughter was sick, but that it wasn't serious. This was Tuesday, June 16, 1981. After a few hours the mother called and left a message for me, saying our daughter was worse. So the chief of police took me to the bus station and I caught the next bus for Havana.

"When I got into Havana I went to William Soler in AltaHabana, it was a children's hospital. Soon as I got there I asked about my daughter, the receptionist said she hasn't arrived yet, I was so anxious. Then I took the bus to Hijas de Galicia hospital which is close to where my daughter lived, thinking she might be there. By the time I got there the doctors there had ordered my daughter to the Soler hospital, where they thought she'd get better care. So then I had to get back to that hospital, you can imagine how I was feeling, wasting time between the two hospitals still not knowing anything about my daughter. I was getting angry and frightened at the same time.

"I got back to the Soler hospital, it was in the afternoon by now, so finally I was able to talk to a doctor, and the mother was there as well. She told me our daughter was already in a coma, she was so bad she couldn't be saved. I asked to see my daughter, I saw her a few minutes before she died. Just a few minutes.

"She went into a coma so fast. They investigated the cause of the disease and they determined she had Dengue. She was only eight years old. She was a good girl, very educated. She loved ballet and was one of the best students in class. She was a real talent in ballet. She was scheduled to go to Germany to dance with a group. I remember that's all she talked about, she was so excited about the trip."

He pauses momentarily to collect this rush of memories. Slowly he speaks of his current life.

"After, I came to live permanently in Colon. I've remarried since, I have three sons, who all live in Colon. And I had another younger daughter from the mother, Lideismy, 30, she also has a daughter. So we have a family here, but always there is this feeling of something missing."

The tone turns from sadness to anger when Edilfredo discusses how the disease was introduced to Cuba.

"It was years later that I found out that Dengue was introduced into Cuba as part of biological terrorism. It was when the government started talking about it and gave the proof. I was outraged to find this. My daughter died, she was a child, she wasn't political, she wasn't a threat, she was just a beautiful little girl who loved ballet. What was her fault? It impacted me greatly, to think that there were people paid money to kill children and to do this crime against humanity. What fault did these children have, what political issue do they have?

"Really, it's such a pain that you keep inside, always. If you let yourself be driven by your impulse you'd kill them, those that did this, but even if you killed them you can't recover your daughter, so there's no point." He hangs his head in his large, rough hands.

"It is difficult to answer these questions, to talk about this. I still miss my daughter. I only have pictures of her now. It is a part of my life, a piece of myself has been taken away from me."

TOBACCO FUNGUS

For centuries the symbol of Cuba has been those wondrous brown leaves rolled expertly into a sensuous smoking experience.

What makes the Cuban *puros* so well regarded is a combination of soil, climate, variety and the culture of growing that comes from experience handed down from generation to generation. The area considered to be the finest growing lands is known as Vuelta Abajo, the dark soiled region located west of Pinar Del Rio city, approximately 150 kilometers from Havana. Encompassing thousands of acres and hundreds of individual tobacco growers, the most famous of these farms is the Robaina plantation near the town of San Luis. Stretching back to 1845, the Robainas are known as the suppliers of the best of the best. Consistently, more than 80 percent of their leaves are used as cigar wrappers, the most demanding and essential part. That amount is compared to an average 35 percent from most other tobacco fields.

The reputation continues with the current keeper of the faith, Don Alejandro, probably the most famous of them all. This energetic, genial master grower, having past his 90th year, was given the ultimate honor by having a brand of cigars named after him more than a decade ago. He's reached the status of living legend, as tourists from around the world make the trek to his home to catch a glimpse, maybe even to talk to the maestro. Most are content to walk through the homestead that is set up as homage to his profession and a living display to the thousands of gifts he's received from worldwide admirers.

These days Don Alejandro's time is taken up more with the devotees than with the operation of the farm. He is simply incapable of being inhospitable—he never misses the opportunity to greet and talk to all those who come out to see the legend and his land.

While his expertise is in the growth of the tobacco leaf, he also has intimate knowledge of the time when the harvests were being destroyed by a tobacco fungus blamed on Cuban-American pilots from Florida. The attack in the late 1970s devastated the crop and to this day continues to cost the Cuban government millions in control measures.

A second attempt to wipe out his crop took place in 1999. His farm was specifically targeted for the spraying of a biochemical chemical that would have destroyed his produce, his livelihood and maybe his life. If not for a quick thinking counter-agent, the plan would have succeeded.

DON ALEJANDRO ROBAINA

Despite his age, Don Alejandro Robaina has conceded little. He still wakes up early in the morning, makes sure all is running smoothly on the *finca*, doles out responsibilities, meets and greets dozens of tourists, expends all sorts of energy without stop, and still enjoys close to a dozen cigars, often with fine Cuban rum, daily.

Don Alejandro Robaina

The one compromise he does allow—"I don't work as hard as before, I have my grandson running the place on a daily basis now, so I don't do nearly as much as before."

Don Alejandro is the latest in the long line of the Robaina legacy that dates back to 1845.

He greets his visitors with a large grin and firm handshake, showing them into a secluded salon set up for his favorite pastime, which he shortly indulges in, as he pulls an *esplendido* sized puro from his shirt, sits down on the plush leather chair, and expertly puts flame to leaf.

Before a question is asked, Don Alejandro grabs a plastic framed photo from the bar. There are three men in the picture, a crop duster plane in the background, and a signed note on the upper left corner. It is proof, he says, of the chemical warfare against Cuban tobacco production, and the series of coincidences that saved his crop.

"You know who this is?" He points to the large smiling man with the baseball cap. "This is José Basulto, of the Brothers to the Rescue."

Basulto headed the organization that in the mid 1990s conducted a series of rescue operations to pick up Cuban rafters in the Florida

Framed photo from Don Alejandro Robaina showing Brothers to Rescue head José Basulto (with cap), arm around Pedro Juan Pablo Roque. René González kneeling.

Straits. The operation turned into illegal over-flights into Cuban airspace, including a number of incursions above Havana. In all more than twelve incidents were documented by the Cuban government, each one protested to American and international aviation authorities. United States officials did nothing to curtail the flights. The Cuban government had previous experiences with small civilian planes from America dropping suspected biochemical agents on Cuban soil, and while the Brothers to the Rescue were initially dropping anti-government leaflets, there were also indications that the group was working on dropping bombs.

With the illegal flights continuing, the government threatened to shoot down the planes the next time they violated Cuban airspace. In February 1996 two planes were brought down; a third, with Basulto piloting at low altitude, made its way back to Florida. There remains controversy to this day as to the exact location where the planes were intercepted, with the Brothers claiming they were fired upon over international waters. There has been no denial from the Brothers to the Rescue as to the frequency of their illegal flights over Cuba. The result of the incident was the passage of the Helms-Burton Act which strengthened the American embargo against Cuba.

Basulto has been accused of a number of terrorist acts against Cuba, including taking a boat to Cuba to fire a cannon at a hotel in 1962. Basulto spoke of the act under oath during the trial of the Cuban Five in 2001, although no charges have ever been laid against him. Lawyer and civil rights activist Leonard Weinglass says Basulto's action was a clear violation of the Neutrality Act. Weinglass is currently representing Antonio Guerrero, one of the Cuban Five.

The photo in Don Alejandro's possession shows Basulto with his arm around Pedro Juan Pablo Roque, a Cuban-American who turned out to be a double agent. Also in the picture is René González, a Cuban arrested for infiltrating anti-Castro organizations in Miami. He is one of the Cuban Five currently serving long jail sentences. Behind the three is a small crop duster.

According to Don Alejandro, Pedro was "considered as a son," to Basulto. The two also worked together, and one of the assignments Pedro was given was to spray the tobacco crops of Robaina. What Basulto didn't know, however, was that Pedro was a close friend of Robaina, as well as a double agent.

"Pedro worked here on the farm when he was younger. He was like most young Cubans, they had time to work in the country for a few weeks in the summer. Pedro was a very good person, he worked hard and I got to know him well. What I didn't know was later he went to Miami to infiltrate these Cuban-American terrorist organizations in order to prevent terrorist attacks against us."

Pedro took his order from Basulto, flew the plane (the one in the photo) over Cuban airspace and sprayed Robaina's crop. The spray, however, was not the deadly thrips palmi which quickly destroys the crop, but a harmless chemical Pedro substituted. He returned to Basulto to report on the success. Shortly after he was forced to flee Miami when his Cuban compatriots, including René González, were taken into custody by American government officials.

"So there is proof that these terrorists did try to destroy my crops," Robaina says. "They didn't succeed because of the luck of having Pedro, but in so many other areas they did spread the disease and devastated such an important economic industry in Cuba."

While that attempt failed, Cuba tobacco did suffer devastating attacks years earlier. "It was in around 1979–1980. Almost all the tobacco fields in Pinar Del Rio province were destroyed. This is the most important area for tobacco in Cuba. Approximately 90 percent of the total crop was affected by a fungus never before seen in Cuba. People who had late plantings escaped the worst of it, but that was only a few farmers. The rest had their crops destroyed."

Robaina takes a long, deep pull on his cigar, the smoke rising slowly from the perfectly shaped ash-white tip. He feels comfortable with his life and the passing of his inheritance to the younger generation, not that he's in any hurry to leave.[10]

"We've been here since 1845, the history here is more important than anything else."

Robaina started smoking at the age of ten. "I know it's not healthy, but it's less harmful than drugs or cigarettes. The custom these days is to stop smoking, but at my age I have no intention to quit. I've been all around the world, so many countries are banning smoking and cigars have a bad reputation, but for me it has been my life. There is nothing better than a cigar and some Cuban rum. I don't think cigar smoking will ever end, maybe cigarettes some day, but cigars are more cultured, more refined. It will never go out of style."

While he finds his family name on an elite brand of Cuban cigars to be a great honor, the fact that other cigar companies outside Cuba are starting to copy the Robaina brand is a deep insult. "There is only one Cuban tobacco, and it is the best in the world. When other cigar companies outside Cuba try to fool people into thinking this cigar is from Cuba, and it's not, that is wrong. And especially I don't like it if they try to put my name or face on a cigar that did not come from my crops. It is not right.

"I've had fights with stores who are selling fake cigars, because Cuba has suffered most from this, our reputation is suffering because people smoke bad cigars and they think they're from Cuba."

SWINE FEVER

Of all the biological agents introduced to Cuba, probably the cruelest was the swine fever that hit in 1971. For the Cuban people, few things are more important than pork—and they demonstrate this in so many wonderfully delectable ways. Whether the traditional roasted pig over an open pit, to the more exotic smoked cutlets, nothing comes close to the culinary love affair Cubans have with pork.

But for almost five years the population had to do without the sweet meat. Things were so bad that young children grew up with no idea what a pig even looked like, with teachers and parents resorting to showing them photos as a remembrance of better dietary days.

One of the areas hardest hit by the fever was the Pinar Del Rio province, west of Havana. The location, better known for growing the country's best tobacco, is also home to wide acres of sugar cane, timber, and pork production.

In less than six months the swine fever resulted in the slaughter of more than 500,000 pigs nation wide, burned and buried in a drastic attempt to control the disease. The effort was successful, but then it took those long lean years before the government was confident enough to introduce a new stock into the countryside.

ISRAEL GONZÁLEZ FERRO

Israel and his family live in one of the highest points of the Sierra de los Organos mountains, north of the town of San Cristobal, in the Pinar Del Rio area. It is a rugged land, with its deep valleys and steep ranges. The long narrow roads are paved and well maintained, connecting in a winding, haphazard fashion from farm to farm. The views are spectacular, and despite the remoteness, the farmers enjoy running water, electricity, close-by medical and educational facilities, and the ability to make a decent living from their work. This is where the revolution survives, and thrives.

The González family runs a farm of approximately 150 pigs. They have lived on this land since well before the revolution, and it is expected that the farming tradition will be handed down for generations to come.

Israel is 76 years old and has the classic appearance of a farmer, to the point of cliché—thin, scruffy, unshaven. He is also unhesitatingly friendly, eager to talk of his life and anxious to be the proper host. Coffee, juice and an abundance of fresh fruit picked from the variety of pear, papaya and mango trees on his land is readily offered.

His remembrance of the swine fever that wiped out his stock still comes with a combination of anger and disgust.

"I was one of the biggest farmers in the area when the swine fever hit. At that time I had over 200 pigs. We had a contract with the government to sell our pigs, and we could eat as many as we wanted to for personal use. The fever hit all of a sudden, it was totally unexpected, this had never happened before and there was no natural reason for it. We found out later that it appeared the fever was brought into Cuba intentionally."

Israel González Ferro

Shaking his head at the idea of the fever being introduced by human hands, Israel vividly recalls how devastating the disease was.

"The pigs would start to get sick, the tail is always curled, when they got sick it became straight, they had fever, diarrhea. When the government realized the pigs were sick they had to kill them all, immediately. In a second they knew there was a problem, they knew how quickly this disease could spread and they had to deal with it immediately. Trenches were built by bulldozers, the pigs were killed, set fire to and covered up. It was a very serious situation. It was a disaster for the province, as this is one of the prime pig farming areas in Cuba. In this small area alone there were more than 3,000 pigs killed. Everyone was so upset, they knew what it would mean to us economically, and to our diet."

It was a terrible time, Israel recalls, not just for his personal business, but for the impact it had on the Cuban palate.

"We Cubans love to eat pork, it is the most popular meat for us. Not to have it for almost five years, it was a cruel punishment. We'd raise chickens during that time. But it's not the same, the Cuban people love to eat pork, and there was none to be had in the country. Nothing. So finally, after they thought it was safe, we started bringing pigs in from Canada, various breeds."

With his pig farm operation shut down for years, Israel had to find other ways to support his family.

"We started working in the fields, cutting cane, tobacco, other things. All the while no pigs, no pork to eat. It affected so many people, not just me, but the other workers, the government, the people who eat pork. It was a terrible thing to have happen," he speaks of this seriously, but then pauses, raises his eyes and breaks out into a big grin.

"I can laugh about it now, because you can't imagine people being so desperate just because there was no pork, but at that moment there was no hope, it was devastating. The worst part was that at that time my boys were young, they didn't even know what a pig looked like. We had to show them pictures of a pig for them to know."

He quickly smiles and recalls when he was at last able to eat pork again. "I'd forgotten how pork tasted, so when the first time I ate it again it was incredible, but I remember thinking, what is this meat? It didn't take me long to remember that sweet taste, and I hope I never have to give it up again."

6

Boca de Samá

Throughout the 1960s and 1970s a number of coastal villages came under attack from anti-revolutionary groups of Cuban-Americans originating from Florida. The hundreds of small towns along the 500 miles of northern shoreline were within close range and made easy targets.

A well-known incident occurred with the murder of the Romero family in Altamira, in the Escambray region of central Cuba in late June 1962. During the attack Paula Romero, her sister Teodora and their mother Vicenta were captured and beaten with rifles. The group then dragged José Pio Romero and his sister Ana Romero from their house, where they were taken into a nearby paddock and shot.

Near the beach resort of Varadero, four children of a family from Bolondrón were brutally murdered in a terrorist attack in the late 1960s. The mother, Nicolas Diaz, told authorities that the attack occurred at 11 p.m. when a group of men demanded entry into their home. Without warning they started shooting and in a matter of minutes Felicia, Gregorio, Fermin, Yolanda and Josefita were killed. Less than a week later a group of Cuban-Americans who had infiltrated the area from Florida were arrested for the crimes.

The most infamous assault came on the night of October 12, 1971 in the tiny hamlet of Boca de Samá, located at the northern tip of Holguin province, in eastern Cuba. Centered in the province is the capital city of Holguin, the second most populated in the country. The city is famous for the 450 steps that lead to the spectacular view on the top of the Loma de la Cruz (Hill of the Cross), site of the annual May pilgrimage in honor of its construction in 1950.

Holguin, founded in 1545, is a vibrant municipality quite unlike Havana. Known as the city of parks, its streets are well laid out in squares, thanks to the military influence of the urban planners. The streets are clean and well maintained, and there is ample evidence that the city is going through an economic resurgence, including the opening of a three-block pedestrian mall, lined with restaurants, shops, clothing stores, bars and hotels. Holguin is less than an hour south of Boca de Samá, and all routes to Boca lead through the city. The village is in a spectacular picturesque location, nestled between the wide mouth of the Samá River and surrounded by lush green hills. It is idyllic, tranquil, and most of the time, safe.

The town of 60 men, women and children was no more than a collection of a dozen small wooden homes, a store and a school when it was attacked by a group of approximately 15 men who left evidence pointing to the anti-Castro terrorist group Alpha 66.[1]

The organization had a long history of activities against Cuban targets. Originated in the early 1960s as part of an invasion against Cuba, Alpha 66 has been tied to a variety of violent acts in America and Cuba. They continue to operate in the Miami area to this day. Its own website states, "Alpha 66 was created with the intention of making commando type attacks on Cuba to maintain the fighting spirit of the Cuban people after the failure of the Bay of Pigs invasion."[2]

Boca de Samá was a prime target not only for its remoteness but for the numerous caves that dot the shoreline—ideal for storing weapons and supplies. Prior to the revolution the area was the site of a number of banana plantations owned by the United Fruit Company, the same corporation that was implicated in the 1954 overthrow of Guatemala president Jacobo Arbenz. The villagers claim that many who took part in the attack were former employees of the company who fled after the revolution.

These days Boca is still a sleepy little village. The shop that was the center of much of the fighting during the attack has been torn down, and a museum built in its place. The wooden homes are all but gone as well, replaced with new concrete structures.

Besides the sale of locally caught fish, the residents of Boca make a living working the land and raising livestock. On rare occasions a few tourists venture their way into town, coming from the near-by resorts at Guardalavaca.

The assault on Boca de Samá was co-ordinated at night, with two boatloads of terrorists landing on the west shore, closest to the village. They were immediately detected, fought their way into the store, all the while spraying bullets into the homes, school, and anything else they could hit. In the process two residents were killed. After a fierce gun battle at the school the attackers (referred to as bandits by most Cubans) retreated back to their landing crafts, making their way to the mother ship which was stationed less than a kilometer away. It all took less than an hour.

NANCY PAVÓN PAVÓN

Nancy Pavón's story is well known in Cuba. She's the 15-year-old girl who survived a harrowing night of terror during the attack on Boca de Samá. With her right foot almost completely shot off, and her younger sister badly injured by the same bullet, Nancy and her family struggled to escape with their lives.

It's a saga that happened more than 30 years ago. Nancy, now in her early 50s, copes with a different kind of horror these days. It is the reality of having to deal with the loss of her foot, the endless physiotherapy, and the understanding that the older she gets, the more she'll have to endure. Nancy has told her story many times, and has appeared often on Cuban radio and television, gaining a small measure of celebrity. She recites the details of the night of terror calmly and quickly, almost to the point of boredom, but also comments repeatedly that she can rarely remember the night without crying. The tears do come, but not until the end.

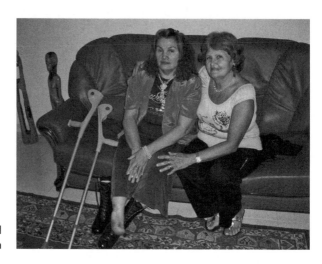

Nancy Pavón and her sister Ziomara

Her sister Ziomara, 61, was attending Nancy during the interview. Ziomara was not with the family during the attack at Boca de Samá. but in Guardalavaca, approximately 30 kilometers away. Her remembrances are intermingled with Nancy's.

Nancy walks with a crutch under each arm, maneuvering awkwardly. She lowers herself slowly onto a long leather couch. She is a large woman, not obese, and admits needing to lose a few pounds. Wearing a well fitting dress and carefully prepared make-up, she looks somewhat older than her 51 years.

She rubs her right leg immediately upon sitting, quickly removes her prosthesis and shows, with a strange sense of pride bordering on smugness, the stump of flesh at the end of her leg. Nancy's right foot was almost completely torn off during the attack. But she now complains good heartedly about waiting for something she can't do without.

"I've been expecting a new prosthesis for my foot, it takes longer than usual because it's hard to get the materials, the embargo makes it more difficult to get things, even things like this."

With a sigh and a smile she starts to recount the details of that night in 1971, starting with the portion that always excites her to anger.

"The bandits who attacked boasted of what they did, they were treated like heroes in Miami and when they got back they told everyone they killed lots of people, destroyed the town, all sorts of things that weren't true. They attacked, but didn't do as much damage as they claimed.

"I was born in Boca. I had just turned 15 a few months before the attack, in July 1971. The 15th birthday is a big celebration for Cuban girls, it is a celebration for them turning into a woman. My mother had a sick aunt so we didn't celebrate my 15th in July. We were making plans to do something, but nothing happened. After the attack I didn't want to do anything like that. I couldn't. My other sister, Angela, was also injured. She was 13 at the time. She doesn't do interviews like this, she is still so affected. She just doesn't want to remember.

"The day of the attack, we were both going to school. We were doing our homework, it was at night. Maybe around 9, or 9:30. That evening we finished our homework and we were in bed. My father, Bienvenido, was going to bed early, he had a toothache. He was part of the Cuban frontier guard, a civil group that helped keep watch on the coast. When he got up to take something for his toothache, he heard machine gun fire. He went out to go to the little village, it's about a kilometer away from our house. I remember it was a quiet night, cloudy. Very dark. It was not too hot, but we had the windows open.

"We lived in a small home up on a hill overlooking the town. Standing from the hill you could see everything. The dirt road passed just by our house and went into the village. It was just a small place, maybe 15, 16 homes. One store, a pharmacy, some place to buy groceries, not much else. The village had nothing militarily, no base, nothing.

"When my father went out the door he noticed the attack. They fired and they fired, and then they fired an illuminating explosion, it lit up the whole area and in the light they saw my father run back into the house.

"There were two boatloads of bandits and they scattered over the town, dropping pamphlets, anti-Castro pamphlets. They had a mortar with them and they fired it and it hit the hill, close to our house. My father ran back into our home and they started shooting at him, one of the bullets passed by his head, it missed him by just a few inches. It came so close it made him dizzy. He told my mom to wake up the children, he said there's an attack on the town.

"My sister Angela was still sleeping, I woke up and jumped over my sister to protect her. I started putting on my shoes and then I screamed, 'I'm dead.' I felt something hit me, I don't know where, but something hit me. It hurt, but I didn't notice where the pain came from, I was too scared. It was dark in the house and I couldn't tell what had happened to me, but I knew I had been shot. At the same time my sister also cried out, 'I'm dead too.'

"My father yelled back at us, 'You can't be dead, you are both still talking. You're not dead.' That's how kids think, you know they don't know what being dead is. We felt pain and we assumed we were dead. All this time we were hearing the shots coming in through the house; whizzing by us, hitting furniture and glasses and making zing and zipping sounds.

"My mother, her name is Francisca. They both are alive, in their 80s, and still live in Boca. She started yelling at everyone to get out the back way of the house. I started to get up and that's when I realized my right foot was almost completely shot off. It was hanging by a thread. I felt down to touch it and I felt the blood, my leg was wet with blood. My left foot was hit as well. It was the same bullet that hit both feet, almost shooting off my right foot and then hitting my left. It was a 50 caliber bullet, they told me later.

"Incredibly, it was the same bullet that hit my sister in her foot. I'm sure it was her left foot. This one bullet did all this damage to me and

my sister. It was a miracle it didn't kill me, because for just a little bit
this bullet almost hit my head. I was bending down to put on my right
shoe, I just lifted my head and at that moment the bullet struck. If I
was still bending down I'd have been killed."

Nancy pauses for a moment to collect her breath and her thoughts.
She blinks rapidly but is not crying. When asked what happened to the
shoe for her right foot, she opens her eyes wide and smiles.

"That shoe was left in the house. After it was all over, when we
returned, the shoe was still there. My father said it was still white,
no blood on it at all. The rest of the house, it was terrible, so many
bullet holes in it, so many things broken. So much blood on the floor
and the walls. There was the skin of both mine and my sister's foot
stuck to the mosquito nets. They counted 25 bullets. One of the bullets
went through a can of kerosene we had in the house, fortunately the
can was not filled, there was only one or two inches of kerosene in
the can; the bullet passed through above where the kerosene was, so
it didn't explode. The house was in such bad shape the government
tore it down and built a new one for us, just a little bit down from the
location of the original house on the hill. It still overlooks the village.
My parents still live there."

Nancy shifts herself slightly, rubbing the top of her thigh slowly,
in an effort to ease the pain that shows on her face. She retraces the
details of the events leading to her being shot.

"These bandits landed in town and were tossing out propaganda
sheets. They caught my uncle and tied him up, they called him by name,
they knew him. So we all thought these terrorists lived in the area
before the revolution. There were about twelve bandits in two boats.
They also broke into the store and destroyed it completely. They shot
up all the milk bottles for the babies. Later the store was turned into
a museum with displays from that night and the history of the area.

"During the first few minutes a fisherman happened to go by and
he saw what was going on and he went to get help. By this time the
chief of the station confronted these bandits and they shot him eight

times in the legs. But they didn't kill him, he survived and he still lives in Boca. Carlos Andrés Escalante, it was a miracle he survived. They did kill two people, though, and injured others."

Nancy's sister Ziomara, sitting next to her on the couch, pointedly adds her opinion as to the identity of the attackers, "In this place, there were two of them who lived in Boca and then went to Miami after the revolution. That's why they picked Boca, they knew the place. They knew the people. How else could they know the names of the people, calling them out by name? They knew it would be an easy place to attack. That it was defenseless."

Nancy expands on the political background of the Boca de Samá region.

"My father was also helpful to the revolutionaries, so maybe that was why they attacked. These people were affected by the revolution, they left property. But to kill innocent people, to shoot up the town and do what they did, that's terrorism. There is no justification to do what they did, to shoot and kill farmers and children."

She then returns to the story of her flight from the attack. "We were all still in our house. I was bleeding badly from my leg, there was blood all over my clothes. Someone put me on the kitchen table, it must have been my father. I could still see the bullets coming into the house, passing by me. I don't remember if I felt the pain, I think everyone was so scared. I was crying, but not yelling. I remember my sister screaming and crying, she was hurt in her foot, and it was bleeding badly also.

"My father said we had to get out of the house and get to the road at the back. We could hear the bandits still shooting, but there were townspeople shooting back. And one of the bandits was injured, we could hear him, "Don't leave me." Then some of the bandits started to leave, but at the time we didn't know, we still thought they were coming to get us. My father carried me and my sister out of the house and to the back. We got to the road and we sat there. In total there were eight people—my parents, me and my sister, and three other brothers. And a daughter of one of my brothers, she was only three years old.

It was so dark, it was such a dark night. The little one got lost, she wandered off and no one saw her. So my father went to look for her, to try and find her in the darkness. My sister and me we decided not to stay, we started to run a half-kilometer to a neighbor's house. We didn't want to stay there and be killed.

"So I ran, with my one good foot and the other one hanging off my leg. My sister helped me run with her, we fell many times. It was a struggle to go just a few steps before I had to stop. I was falling all the time and we were so scared. We ran that way towards the house of our neighbor. The road was muddy and full of stones, my left foot was covered in mud, mixed in with the blood, and it hurt from the bullet wound. My good foot was getting torn up with the stones and mud. My other leg, it was still bleeding, and it was covered in dirt as well, and that foot was just being dragged behind. It was terrible." She pauses again to recover, her eyes moist and narrow.

"My father came back, he found the young one, and saw we were gone. But he found the trail of blood and followed. When we arrived at the other house everyone there tried to get some bed sheets to control the bleeding. We could all still hear the shootings, they were still shooting their guns and we could hear the bullets." Nancy pauses again to take a deep breath. "I don't know why I'm not crying now, I usually cry when I tell this part. It's hard, so difficult to remember these things.

"The neighbor told my father to take us all to a nearby cave, to hide there so the bandits wouldn't kill us. But he said no, he has to get us to a hospital because he was afraid I'd bleed to death. So he carried me and my sister, it was five kilometers to find more help at the frontier guard station. The bullets were still flying by, we were crying and screaming and my father was covered in blood and mud. Finally about one kilometer up the road a jeep was seen coming from the station. The jeep stopped and one of the guards saw us and asked what happened.

"My father yelled to the frontier guard, 'Look at my daughters, they are bleeding to death. Help my daughters, they are going to die.' The men in the jeep said we had to go to the closest hospital, in Banes, which was 38 kilometers away. We got to the Banes hospital and afterwards my father told me—that when the doctors saw him they thought he was covered in mud, but it wasn't mud—it was blood, my blood. It was there they took my foot off, they just cut the last piece of flesh still attached. They operated on me twice, the first time there was some problem, with the skin graft. So they had to do another operation.

"My younger sister was more nervous than me, she was afraid she was going to lose her foot. I think it was about two hours from the time we left our house to the time we got to the hospital. I knew they couldn't save my foot. They told me my foot was removed and at that time I was just happy to be alive, I didn't realize how it would affect the rest of my life.

"There were problems when I was in the hospital, I had convulsions during the blood transfusion. The next day they collected me and took me to an ambulance where they transported me to Santiago [approximately three hours away]. For the next ten days or so I started to get weaker and weaker, I was in and out of consciousness while in the hospital, the problem was my reaction to the blood transfusions. After 28 days I was sent to Havana, to the Frank País hospital which specializes in orthopedic surgery. That's when things got worse. I was there for 19 months, and during that time I had six more operations. So many skin grafts, so many complications I thought I'd never get out of there."

Ziomara added that she "remembered those times, there was so much stress. We were all with Nancy and every time they told her she'd have to have another operation, she'd start crying. I couldn't stay in the same room, I couldn't stand to see her cry."

Ziomara continues. "Nancy's other foot, was sliced open, the tendons were exposed. Luckily they were able to save that one. For ten days Nancy was in intensive care. The other sister, yes, she was recovering well. In Santiago. When the other sister finally got in to see Nancy, she was so scared she hid her face under the bed sheets, she didn't want to see her sister in that condition. She couldn't speak to her. It was so close, Nancy was so close to death for so long."

At this time, Nancy can no longer contain her emotions. It is the impact of her sister's remembrances that causes her to start crying softly, steadily, looking down at the floor. Her sister reaches over and gives her a hug.

Nancy picks up the conversation. "They operated on my leg as well, they did two operations at one time, skin transplants. After they sent me back home, then one month later I had to return to the hospital for more operations. It was difficult, very difficult. There was only one doctor there in Havana who said I'll get you to walk, everyone else thought it would be impossible. But I knew I'd walk again."

Despite that strength of character, Nancy admits it has been a long, hard road she's traveled since that horrible night.

"Physically it has taken so much from me, the operations, I have trouble with my leg as well. And now I'm getting infections, so I have to be in the hospital for that. How many operations have I had? I don't know, maybe 15, 20. But mentally it has been just as difficult. I've missed out on so many things. My teenage years were spent mostly in hospitals, and I was never able to do things that others were able to."

Nancy stresses that she can walk on her own, without the use of the crutches. However, she does rely on them extensively, and admits it's getting harder to walk unassisted, due to the weight she's put on.

"I'm a bit overweight, but after all I've been through I'm entitled to," it is said with a smile, and a small sense of embarrassment. "I promised myself that I would lose a few pounds. Now, every six months I have to change the prosthesis, but it is so hard to get new ones because of the blockade. I have had infection problems lately; the prosthesis rubs against my leg and the older I get the harder it is. But I know that this is something I will have to live with for the rest of my life."

Nancy, who is divorced with three children and one grandchild, sadly reflects on how her life was forever altered in a span of a few seconds.

"I'm constantly thinking of this, every step I take reminds me of that night and how quickly that one bullet changed my life, and the life of my sister and family. My family, and my children suffer along with me. This can happen to anyone, but only I know exactly how I feel, what it has meant to my life, what I have gone through. But I'm very proud otherwise, I don't know what would have happened to me if not for the support I get from the government, they pay for the hotel, the hospital, all the treatment I get. I'm very proud of that."

Despite the hard times, she is far from pessimistic. "When I lost my foot and came back to my house in Boca, in 1973 or 1974, I registered at the frontier guard. I climbed the old wooden watch tower, I could see boats way off in the distance. I thought about whether they were more terrorists or not. I wanted to join the guard, to feel I was doing something positive. Everyone was nervous of me climbing that tower, but I wanted to do it. I wanted to show I could still do things, not to let this defeat me.

"I miss my foot, but my hands are fine."

CARLOS ANDRÉS ESCALANTE GOMEZ

He goes by the nickname Chino, in reference to his Oriental ancestry. But Carlos Andrés Escalante Gomez has also been called "lucky" on more than one occasion by those who have heard his story.

Chino, 63, has lived in this small village for more than 45 years. He's considered to be the area's unofficial historian and has gained more than a little bit of local notoriety for his exploits on the night of the attack.

Chino is more than happy to recall the details of the night the terrorists came. "It was around 6 p.m., dusk, there was a vessel we could see on the horizon. Most everyone thought it was just a boat, but it was a little suspicious; because it was moving along the horizon, and most boats move north to south when they pass by.

"When it became dark, we could only hear the noise of the boat, it had a very powerful engine, it kept passing back and forth along the coast. The village was completely dark, there was an electrical plant that supplied lights to the village and homes, but it was under repair."

Chino relates that the residents of Boca de Samá had good reason to be wary of this vessel.

Carlos Andrés Escalante Gomez
at the museum in Boca de Samá

"Everyone was keeping quiet, we had a previous experience with this kind of thing. One year before, in September 1970 a boatload of bandits, we were told they were also from Alpha 66, landed here, they landed five kilometers way, they went inland, and made it close to Santiago, which is about 150 kilometers away. The bandits were killed there. They didn't do any harm to our village. After that incident the authorities increased security and advised us to keep alert. I was head of the Coast Guard at Boca de Samá.

"Around 8 p.m. a security officer visited me and updated what the boat was doing. We decided to go closer to the coast, there are a series of caves along the shoreline and we thought we should be doing a search around that area. We were in this cave still trying to figure out what the boat was doing, when suddenly a fisherman came running along the coast yelling, he was screaming at the top of his lungs, that he saw a group of people. Immediately we went to look for them, we went running to the school to organize ourselves, in groups of three, and we heard this noise, the bandits were in the town already—they were breaking down the door of the store. The school is just across from the store, maybe ten meters. The three of us in my group ran out of the school. I was out in front and the other two were at my side. We knew there were some of these bandits in the store. We could hear them tearing things up. Afterwards we estimated about 14 of these terrorists attacked the town, and I think there were four or five in the store."

Chino explains that the store had a main front door, with a small side entrance to the left. It was decided that the best approach would be for him to take the side entrance, while his two *compañeros* circled the store on either side.

"When we arrived at the store, I came to the side door and shouted out for those inside to surrender. I was in front of this door, I had a pistol and I pointed the gun at the man inside the store, who was just on the other side of the door. The bandit had a machine gun, and he poked the gun through the door slats and started firing, blindly. It sounded like 100 shots were being fired. He shot me eight times, all of them hitting around my legs, and I immediately fell to the ground. I knew I had been hit, the pain was intense and I could feel my pants soaked with blood."

He states emphatically that even while on the ground, bleeding profusely and in extreme pain, "I kept firing my pistol at these bandits, even when I was lying there, I was only thinking about stopping those bastards."

The other two members of his group were also firing into the wooden store, and by this time the invaders had decided to make a run for it back to the boat.

"After the first shots they all ran away, they took their small boats they landed on and made it back to the big mother ship. When these bandits left the village and they went to the main boat, they started machine gunning the whole town. Every home was shot up, the store, the school, everything. When the terrorists were in town, that's when they killed the two—Lidio Rivaflecha and Ramón Arturo Siam."

Once the shooting stopped it was time to help the wounded.

"The neighbors came out onto the street after the shooting ended, and one of them found me on the ground bleeding, by this time my legs were numb. Maybe I was going into shock, or from the loss of blood. When they got me home they started to clean me up, and they examined all the bullet holes. They took me to a hospital, where I was there for two months recovering.

"One of the bullets hit very close to the artery, if it did I'd have died. All the bullets passed through my legs, five hit my left leg, three hit my right. If the bandit had his machine gun pointed a little higher it would have hit me across my stomach, and that would have killed me for sure. Later a few people went back to the store and they found the bullets on the ground—the same ones that went through me."

Chino is quick to lift his pants leg and show the still visible bullet marks, making a circular pattern from just above his knees to just a few inches below his thigh. "It still causes me pain when I walk, I'll have that for the rest of my life."

It didn't take government officials long to blame those responsible for the attack. As Chino says, there was no attempt to conceal who they were.

"There are many items that prove these attacks came from Miami. The bandits were from Alpha 66, the Miami terrorist group. They left propaganda leaflets behind with their name on them; they hoisted the Alpha 66 flag on one of the trees, and they left a lot of other things that showed where they came from. The day after, reports from Miami described the attack and the group who did it."

Chino says it's not hard to understand why Boca de Samá was targeted. "It's our geographic location, it's not far from the United States and there are many caves here so it's easy for the bandits to hide. My other opinion why they attacked—they had to justify the money that was raised for Alpha 66, they had to act on something, so they attacked a small defenseless village. They didn't have the courage to attack a military post, they just attacked something weak. They brought lots of war equipment like they were going to be here for a long time, but there is no military objective to Boca de Samá, no economic objective. They just wanted to terrorize the people."

According to Chino they did a good job at that.

"Every night after the attack all the parents would take their children and sleep in the woods. That's why the government built the new houses, the cement ones, otherwise everyone would have left the village, the old wooden huts were all shot up and in bad condition. What a terrible thing to experience, everyone was scared to death for months after."

JOSÉ ABEL ROMERO GONZÁLEZ

José is an affable, intelligent man in his mid 60s who conjures up the image of what a country teacher should be—mild-mannered, articulate and deliberate. For years he was the only instructor at Boca de Samá's lone school, educating all his charges from the first grade till they were ready to move on to high school. He was there the night of the attack.

"At that time, in the early 1970s, there was a room on the side of the school that was set aside for where the teacher lived, that was my house. I had running water, a small sink, bathroom, kitchen, living room and a bedroom. It was comfortable for me and for my wife."

José recalls how he came to be assigned to the tiny village of Boca de Samá.

"I graduated in Havana as a teacher in 1969, I was newly wed and there was a person in charge who gave me the assignment here. I had another job proposal to stay in Havana but I came here happy, my wife wanted to come here as well. We both knew where Boca de Samá was, and we both liked living in the country. So we moved here on January 16, 1971. And we've been here ever since.

"The night of the attack it was very dark. One of Nancy's brothers was here with us at the school. When we heard the noise—at the time my wife was seven months pregnant—we first thought it was a fishing boat; we couldn't see anything. A few minutes later we heard people running and shots being fired. We heard men shouting and then we heard the store being smashed up. The school was very close to the store, maybe ten meters. Nancy's brother ran out of the school and went back to his house, up on the hill. We found out later what had happened to Nancy and the ordeal she went through."

José Abel Romero González
outside the school in
Boca de Samá

José, who retired from teaching in 2003, continues. "Next day we found some bullets in the school, and there were at least two bullet marks on the side and a few at the end where we were living. I found one in the closet. It was about 20 minutes of straight shooting. The whole village was shot up, there wasn't one home that didn't have bullet marks on it."

José distinctly recalls hearing a familiar voice calling out in the night.

"When the bandits attacked, there were a few in the store. We heard firing from the store and then we heard Chino yelling, he was cursing and saying some nasty things to the bandits, who were running away. We didn't know what had happened to Chino, we didn't know how badly he was shot up. To have survived that, it was incredible.

"There was this moment of shock and surprise, no one knew what was happening because it was so dark, all the gunfire it was very confusing. Suddenly I heard someone coming and knock on the door, my wife was very afraid and held me back, she wouldn't let me answer the door. We both left through the back door, and at that time the chief of police came up to us and asked where Chino was, because he was head of the coast guard. We told him we heard Chino yelling and we thought he was hurt, but we didn't know exactly where he was. That police officer recognized my voice, otherwise he would have shot me, it was so dark you couldn't see anyone. So he asked what happened and I guess it wasn't long afterwards they found Chino, lying on the ground at the store."

With Chino taken care of, José then had to direct police to the body of one of the murdered villagers.

"I heard Ramón [Siam] fall, I could hear him yell, then shots being fired, then nothing. The police thought only one of the people here had been killed, Lidio [Rivaflecha] but I heard someone moaning at the other side of the village; they lit up the area and found Ramón; blood was pouring out of his mouth, he was slumped over a fence. Murdered in cold blood."

The following day José had to make sure all his students were safe, and then try to explain that night of horror.

"For three days afterwards no one went to school, the children were so afraid. I remember speaking to the children, trying to help them understand what had happened, why these men came here to shoot up the village and to kill people. The approach I took was to analyze why we were the ones attacked—I told the children it was not their fault. Children that age always try to rationalize bad things by blaming themselves, and I emphasized they had no blame in this matter.

"I used the comparison of the assault on the Moncada garrison[3] and the Boca de Samá attack, which was against a defenseless, small village. The Miami media was telling everyone what a great battle it was, that this was a huge industrial area, that we had a radio station, all these things that were just lies. The group that attacked us, Alpha 66, went back to Miami boasting of what a victory they achieved, by doing what, shooting up a little village filled with terrified people? I tried to make the comparison between the Moncada garrison attack and what happened in Boca, what type of men would attack a defenseless village, as opposed to those who attacked a military installation. These people have no ideals, they did it to justify their acts of terrorism, they never went to a fort—they attacked the innocent and the weak, and they still do it."

Like most everyone else in the village, the attack had a long term effect on José and his wife.

"After any noise we heard, even the waves on the ocean, made us afraid. And a few months later some boats passed by, just to terrorize us again. It was about a month after the attack. Nobody's ever tried anything after that, but you always wonder."

7
Caibarién and the Fishermen

Caibarién is a medium sized fishing community approximately 350 kilometers east of Havana, on the north coast of the Archipelago de Sabana-Camagüey. The town's most famous landmark is a ten-foot, five ton gray cement crab that stands guard at the entrance of the main road, welcoming visitors and marking it as an important commercial center.

The area also presents itself as the gateway to some of the newest tourist locations in Cuba—Cayo Santa Maria, Cayo Ensenacho and Cayo Las Brujas. The individual Keys are connected to Cuba's longest causeways, some up to 50 kilometers. These impressive seawater roadways were built in the 1990s and lead to many of the most luxurious hotels on the island. Few tourists make their way to Caibarién, however, having little reason to stray from their all inclusive accommodations.

The town of 80,000 was founded in the early nineteenth century and many of the thin wooden row homes date back to that era. The government built a number of concrete residences approximately 20 years ago, specifically to house the more than 150 fishing families. Caibarién was founded on the fishing industry, and now contains the largest lobster factory in Cuba, helped financially by a number of Japanese enterprises.

Transportation down the narrow streets is accomplished almost exclusively by bicycles or horse—even the taxis use non-gasoline power to maneuver around the dilapidated avenues. Cars are rare, public transit buses pass through infrequently, and anyone driving has to be skilled enough to navigate the bikes, horses and pedestrians that clog the roads.

Besides its fame for fresh seafood, Caibarién is also known, less fortunately, as the target of a number of terrorist acts during the past 30 years. The town is located in the southern point of a triangle that includes the Bahamas to the north-east and Florida directly north. Miami and south Florida are only a few hours away by boat. Prior to the revolution the location proved to be an advantage, with contraband flowing continually from various points in south Florida to the town. Caibarién, so far from Havana and other major centers, was the perfect location for Americans to run from Florida with clothes, goods and other materials, and the Cubans would return the favor with rum, sugar and cigars.

After the revolution the position wasn't quite as advantageous. The town's location proved to be a natural attraction for attacks from south Florida, this time by Cuban-American organizations. Local officials allege some of the first terror operations against Cuba happened here, citing more than 80 acts, including the bombing of the leather factory in the late 1960s.

During the 1970s the Cuban government arranged a contract to allow Cuban fishermen to catch lobster off the southern reefs of the Bahamas. This is where the majority of the actions against Cuban fishermen took place. The Bahamian government prohibited the Cubans from carrying arms to defend themselves, which made them easy prey. Conversely, the Bahamians had no interest in arranging security forces to protect the fishing boats, and would not permit Cuban military to accompany the fishermen.

Caibarién is quiet these days, the attacks now more than 30 years ago. The citizens, however, have not forgotten the past, and in the center square can be found a second-floor museum that details the area's unfortunate experiences with terrorism.

ACACIA PÉREZ VITA

Acacia Pérez Vita has lived all her 70 years in town, and has the typical comportment of those who have been raised in the country—straightforward and dignified. She's had a hard existence that shows in the deep lines that surround her dark eyes, and in her numerous missing teeth. Honest and unemotional, Acacia tells her story as one part of her life, possibly the defining moment, but still just another mark on her journey that is not yet over.

Acacia Pérez Vita at the museum in Caibarién

For a number of years Cuban fishermen were captured, kidnapped and tortured. The only one killed by terrorists was Acacia's husband. There is a small memorial to her husband at the town's museum, where his picture and story are displayed in a simple, nondescript manner.

"His name was Roberto Torna Mirabal. It happened October 4, 1973. He was in the Bahamas area fishing for lobster, under the contract of the Cuban government. I don't know why the Bahamas didn't do it themselves, they were not catching lobster.

"It was a long distance away so these fishermen would go out for ten days at a time. There were usually eleven fishermen on the big ship, and then they'd have two or three smaller boats for the individual men to go out and collect the lobsters. My husband was there for six days and he was coming back; they had fished as much as they could and he was returning when he met another boat, going to the Bahamas. One of his friends in the boat going to the Bahamas asked my husband to come with them, as my husband had just been in that zone and knew the area; knew where to catch the lobster.

"This was October 3 when he met his friend. So my husband decided to go back to the Bahamas. The other fishermen, the ones on my husband's boat, they all returned to Cuba. Nothing happened to them. They came home safely.

"At 1 a.m. on October 4 Roberto met a white boat, according to one of the other fishermen—someone told me this story when they all got back. This white boat, they came up to the fishing boat, and they asked for sugar, rum, cigars. My husband gave these guys some rum and sugar and they asked my husband what he wants in return. Roberto said nothing. The boat then left and no one thought anything more.

"They didn't identify themselves but they seemed to be Cuban, they spoke Spanish and it's easy to tell a Cuban when they talk," she flashes a grin, slowly. She asserts that one Cuban will quickly determine another through speech. "There's a lot of *dichos* [expressions] the Cubans have, their accent. It's easy to know if the person is Cuban or not."

Acacia continues the story by laying the background on how she was told of her husband's unscheduled return to the Bahamas.

"On October 3 at night the manager of the fishing bay came by to let me know that my husband went back to the Bahamas. This was the first time that had happened, but when you're a wife of a fisherman you expect things, and my husband was so helpful a person, when I was told he stayed I just thought that's something he would do.

"That same day a merchant ship in the Gulf of Mexico was attacked. There were other attacks on fishermen going on around this time, so every time he went out I worried. We knew there were some terrorist attacks on fishermen, but the fishermen were not allowed to go armed, it was a treaty with the Bahamas government."

Acacia stops for a moment and taps her fingers on the table. She then suddenly blurts out that, "It wasn't the first time something happened to him, at the time of the Bay of Pigs he was kidnapped, in 1961. In the northern coast he was kidnapped and held on a boat for two days, no food, no water. The boat engine he was forced onto broke down—the terrorists were bringing weapons to Cuba when they captured Roberto. These terrorists were coming to Cuba and their boat died, they came upon my husband's boat and they kidnapped him. They fixed their own boat after two days and they let him go. But he was never afraid, that didn't stop him and he didn't worry about what might happen. But he got back here in bad condition, he came back on April 16 and the Bay of Pigs invasion was April 17."

She then returns to the details of her husband's death. "He suffered from asthma, so he liked to sleep on the top of the ship, the air was fresher and he was able to breathe better. In the middle of the night, this was after the white boat had gone, he heard the sound of an engine so he got up and started to walk towards where he thought the boat was. He didn't have time to say anything, to shout out, they just started firing. He was the only one on top. They shot him dead. He never had a chance. Someone said it was three or four in the morning, maybe later, they were all sure it was the same white boat that came back, the one that was there before. They came back to kill someone. The terrorists boarded the ship and they forced all the crew, about twelve others, to get onto the two smaller boats. Then these people set fire to the larger, main fishing ship. Roberto remained on the main one, dead.

"This was at night, and another Cuban fishing boat saw the fire, it was around 5 a.m. They called the Cuban authorities to warn them this ship was exploding. The government sent planes to search the area to see if they could find the terrorists. They found the boat and the fishermen were picked up, everyone was saved.

"On the morning of October 4 I found out. A fishing industry person came to tell me, 'If you hear about an attack on a fishing boat don't worry, it wasn't your husband's boat.' But then I told him my husband didn't come back with his boat, the *Atun*, he went back to the Bahamas to help a friend on this other vessel, the *Acero 34*. That's when I found out that the boat that was attacked was the same one my husband was on. All the officials came by and there were police and they told me they thought all the fishermen came back OK. But they didn't know my husband was on that one, he wasn't supposed to be there. So I started to fear what had happened. On October 5, there were two people who came to my house, and they gave me the news that my husband was dead."

She switches the interview to the effect her husband's death had on not only her, but the rest of the family.

"I have one daughter, she was 19 at the time, she's 56 now. She was pregnant at the time of her father's death, she was coming home from the hospital to our house here, she didn't know anything. Someone she knew came up to her and told her that her father had been killed. Just like that, no warning, no easy way to tell her. She couldn't handle the shock, she fainted. She was eight months pregnant and had to stay in hospital until she gave birth. My daughter's name is Rita Maria and her child is now 33 years old, Hector is his name. But he never had the chance to know his grandfather."

This was the last assault on the fishing boats as the Cuban side soon after ended the contract with the Bahamas.

"Roberto was such a kind person, he had so many good friends. He loved to play dominos, he was friends with his co-workers, they didn't just work together, they were friends. And he was willing to help anyone. If he wasn't that type of person he may not have gone back to the Bahamas with his friend in the other boat—but he would never turn a friend down."

AMADO JIMÉNEZ RODRÍGUEZ

Amado is a slender man with a classic countenance—strong, deep lines, intense blue-green eyes—it is the face of a person who has spent his life on the sea. He has a half smile and a low voice. If you look hard enough you can still see a thin black line that stretches crookedly from the middle of his neck on the right side, then takes a long L-shaped upward turn.

Amado Jiménez Rodríguez

From the first impression it is apparent he's uncomfortable discussing his near fatal experience; none of the easy welcoming nature that is such a constant characteristic of the average Cuban is forthcoming. He comments a number of times on how hard it is for him to remember that day. He also claims he's been ill for the past week, but later some of his closest acquaintances assert he has a good reputation for liking his drink, and suggest that may be the reason for his hesitancy. Amado is 64 years old. He was 29 when his throat was cut.

"I've been retired for years, I always seem to have a cold or not feel well. I started working on the boats with my father when I was seven or eight years old. This was before the revolution, children that age were expected to work, to earn money for the family. Now, all the kids go to school. It's better. I helped my father who was also a fisherman, and I've always lived in Caibarién. I guess I'll die here too.

"We started fishing lobster in the Bahamas and the day it happened, it was October 12, 1972. We were on our way back to Cuba, we had finished our job. We were resting somewhere because there was bad weather, so it was decided to go into shallow water where the storm wasn't so bad, to protect the boat. Normally we'd go out for ten days, with about twelve or 13 fishermen. The boats were called Cayo Largo, they were big, maybe 60 feet long. Then there were a number of smaller boats that we'd go out in, ten or eleven feet. These small vessels were normally just for one or two people, to collect the lobsters in the traps. The big ship was to hold them until we got back to Cuba.

"So around 11 p.m. that day, these funny guys came around the boat, we were told later they were members of Alpha 66, but to us they were just regular guys. I was asleep, everyone was asleep at that time, there were a few who were sleeping on the top of the boat—it was cooler—and there were others below.

"These guys came onto our ship, and one of them comes to me, I'm asleep, and he cuts my throat. Just like that. That's what wakes me up." Amado recalls it with no change of expression—like he's reading the weather report for the day. In fact, most Cubans react stronger when reading the weather.

"I started bleeding, all night long I was bleeding. I woke up screaming, covered in blood. They grabbed me and told me to shut up or they'd kill me. I thought I was dying. By this time all the other fishermen were awake and trying to understand what was happening. The terrorists had weapons and they pointed them and told everyone to stay calm. These guys were on our boat from 11 p.m. till 6 a.m. I was told by one of the other fishermen they were trying to go back towards

Florida. But they weren't making much headway, so around 6 a.m. they decided to burn our ship. They took me onto their boat and I think they wanted to take me as a hostage back to Miami. I was in and out of consciousness, I knew I was losing a lot of blood and was very weak, so I didn't really understand what was happening. The others were very upset, I was there with my three brothers and my older one starting fighting with these guys, he didn't want them to take me. My brother who started to fight was Juan, my other brothers on the boat were Roque and Plácido."

Slowly, he continues. "So my older brother was fighting them and finally they gave up and tossed me back to the others. They put us all onto the smaller boats, the one we use to go out and collect the lobsters in. These boats are about eleven feet long and are designed for one or two people to work in. But they put us all in two or three, maybe more, all eleven of us, and they put me in one of them alone. I was laid down flat so I could rest, and then the other ones, ten, they were in two or three other of these little boats."

His memory is a little uncertain, but it is finally determined that there were three of the small individual boats, one for him, the other two for five fishermen each. He clarifies things further later.

"You have to know I was not conscious all the time, it's hard for me to remember everything. I was still injured, bleeding, so I don't remember too much of what was happening. I remember lying down in the boat and being very thirsty. It didn't hurt too much, it was like a bee sting, but they said I lost a lot of blood and I was weak. Every time I touched my neck it was wet, I knew I was bleeding badly.

"I do remember that when I was taken to the other boat, one of the terrorists told me, this was an operation to eliminate Castro's fishing fleet. They offended me, they called me a communist, I said OK, I'm a communist, so what? This is your reason for doing this? I didn't talk to them much, the blood didn't allow me to talk too much, and I was weak, but I wanted to let them know what I thought. These people were cowards, attacking an unarmed boat.

"The terrorists didn't leave us much, just a little water and hardly any food. Not nearly enough for us to survive for long. So we would go to the shore and the rocks near the shore where we would collect the rain water. It wasn't much but we did the best we could. Remember these boats were designed for one person to catch lobster. Originally there were eleven people in five boats, I was in one by myself. But these were row boats, so it was very hard to keep all them together, so they decided to get together in two boats, it was easier to stay together and to row them, they didn't get tired as much.

"I remember there were birds near the shore, I can't remember the name of this type of bird. When it's an adult it is bad to eat, the meat is not good. But when these birds are smaller, baby birds, they get bigger but still they can't fly, so they are easy to catch. And the meat is good. They caught some and they cooked it up and made a soup of it, and they gave me some of this. It was very difficult to swallow, but they told me I had to eat something, and the soup was the easiest. I guess that helped save my life. I didn't drink any water, they just put some drops on my lips to keep them moist. I wasn't breathing through my nose or mouth, just through my throat. I think the name of the bird is Corúa, but I don't remember. But when it's a baby bird it's good to eat.

"When we were in the small boats it rained most of the time, the weather was bad. But I remember I liked the rain splashing on my face.

"The government knew we were missing, so they sent out a helicopter to look for us. Another Cuban boat saw ours being burnt, and they informed the authorities. At the same time there was a plane that found us, it was looking for something else, another plane that went down in the area. The plane got help for us, they called back to Nassau and sent a helicopter out and dropped some food and water. This helicopter rescued us and I was taken to Bahamas to be operated on.

"After they let me out of the hospital I returned here and I went out to harvest sugar cane, to recover a bit more. Then after that, I don't know, maybe a few months, all the other fishermen I worked with asked me to come back, to be a fisherman again. My friends didn't want me to retire, and I didn't want to quit fishing. It's in my blood, even if they tried to take my blood out of me, I still had enough to want me to continue to be a fisherman"—it's the only time he allows himself an honest smile during the interview. "I never had any fear of going back, to go back to the same area, they can't make me afraid to stop being a fisherman."

His thoughts move away from the attack and turn to his family. "I was about 27, 28 years old at the time. I was married, I still am, with four children, my wife is still living here—Adelia Córdoba. My children's names are Ramona, Nancy, Amadita, Ernesto. And Roberto. Oh, I have five children," he recovers with a short grin, this one of embarrassment. His wife, who had been listening in the other room, comes over and scolds him for forgetting the number of children he has. He looks down at the floor, sheepishly. "And I have 12 grandchildren, and two great-grandchildren. I don't want to name them all, I can't name them all."

Amado allows himself to reflect on that night he almost lost his life, and the effect it still has on him.

"These people are terrorists, As far as I know they have never been caught, never been punished for what they did to me. I have no idea why they did what they did, I can't imagine a person doing that. You ask me something I can not answer. We were just workers, just doing our job, not bothering anyone. I can't think of the type of person to be able to do that. But it still weighs on me, every day I think of it and try to understand. I was a happier person, with less troubles, before."

8
Literacy Campaign

In the early 1960s the Cuban government developed a series of programs designed to improve the lives of the rural population. One of the most successful was the Literacy Campaign.

The campaign was conducted from mid 1960 to the end of 1961. It involved approximately 100,000 young men and women volunteers, known as the Literary Brigade, who traveled into the countryside to teach those outside the cities to read and write. The average age of the instructors ranged between 15 and 18. Before the revolution literacy rates averaged around 50 percent in the rural areas. By 1962 it was raised to 80 percent. Today Cuba has one of the highest rates in the world, at approximately 95 percent of its total population of 11 million.

During the Literacy Campaign, which targeted more than 1 million Cubans, a number of these young educators were attacked in an effort to undermine the effectiveness of the program. The counter-revolutionaries were based in the mountains of Cuba, spreading terror from Pinar Del Rio to the Escambray and Sierra Maestra mountains.

An estimated 14 teachers were killed during the length of the campaign. Two of the most gruesome incidents included the deaths of Conrado Benitez and Heliodoro Rodriguez. Conrado, 18, was in the Escambray mountains of the south central provinces. He was kidnapped on January 5, 1961 along with his student, the adult farmer Rodriguez.

The two were captured, tortured and killed. A few days after the incident local military forces rounded up a group of Cuban-Americans who confessed they had come from Florida with the intent of spreading terror among the farmers. They knew of the Literacy Campaign and by coincidence came upon Conrado Benitez and his student. One of the accused, Mirio Pérez Venegas, testified to what happened that day—

"It was as if there had been a party in the camp that night. We were all shouting at him [Conrado Benitez] at the same time in the corral, we threw stones at him, we spat, swore and even said to Conrado, 'If you join us we'll spare your life.' But he refused."

Venegas explained what took place afterwards, "First they got hold of Conrado, who had to practically run with the rope around his neck in order not to be dragged, while all those present beat him with sticks and cut him with knives. When he was under the tree chosen for the execution, the rope was thrown over a branch and the teacher looked around... The body was lowered and raised a few times, as if he were a puppet, until he was dead, then we left him hanging there."[1]

An equally horrific incident occurred when teacher Manuel Ascunce Domenech and adult student Pedro Lantigua were killed in the Escambray mountains on November 26, 1961. This became one of the most gruesome attacks against the young teachers, and helped galvanize the Cuban government to end the threat of the terrorists in the mountains.

Co-incidentally, Manuel was teaching under the organizational brigade named in honor of Conrado Benitez.

MARIA DOLORES ASCUNCE

The 61-year-old Maria Dolores Ascunce is a gentle woman, physically slight, almost frail. Her low voice and soft answers are sometimes hard to understand. She gives the impression of having had a difficult, unhappy life. Maria currently lives in Havana.

"My brother Manuel Ascunce was a member of the Literacy Campaign, the name of the brigade he worked under was Conrado

Benitez, who was another teacher murdered in January 1961. My brother was killed November that year.

"My brother was 16 years old. This was in 1961. I was 14 at the time. The campaign was set up by the government, Fidel Castro asked the youth of the country to join these brigades. At that time there was a high percentage of people outside the cities who were illiterate,

Maria Dolores Ascunce

so this was the best way to teach them. The teachers had children's books, school books that taught the alphabet and basic reading skills, non-political books and papers.

"Most of the young people were in secondary school, it was a voluntary program but the response was very positive, there were an estimated 100,000 who signed up. They still had to keep up their own school work, but this gave them a chance to go out to the countryside and help others."

She describes the process of co-ordinating the volunteers. "The teachers at the schools would hand out these forms to those interested in participating in the campaign. My brother took one and brought it home to my parents, who had to give authorization. When my brother told me about this I was sure my father would not agree. My brother had never been outside Havana, but my father signed the form and I remember him telling my brother that it would be hard work, and that the conditions in the country would be difficult. My father thought it was a good program, and my brother was excited to go, he thought it would be an adventure. And he did want to help those people. My mother, I don't think she was too happy to have him go.

"There was never any discussion about the potential dangers, yes by that time there were teachers killed. But I guess my parents didn't consider the danger, they thought my brother would be safe. In May my brother handed in the form, and in June he went to the countryside. He was going to high school, like most of the kids, so they had to adjust the school year and the courses for those who did register. No, I didn't feel jealous of my brother going and missing school. I was 14 years old and didn't fully understand what he was going to do. He was sent to Trinidad to get a list of farms they would be sent to.

"There were terrorists operating there at that time, but no one would think they would attack someone who was simply teaching these farmers how to read and write. Yes it had happened before, but we all thought it was just a rare thing, and they had captured the ones who had killed Conrado.

"The family my brother was hosted to, the father was Pedro Lantigua. My brother was originally in another house, close to a main road, but he switched host families so the co-ordinator of the brigade could be closer to that road. The Lantigua house was further into the countryside, more isolated. My brother was teaching both Pedro and his wife.

"One night, the classes were given at night as the farmers worked during the day, and my brother helped out. One night these bandits came and called out that they were Cuban militia men. So Pedro thought they were with the government, in the area for security. Still, he came out with a rifle, when he opened the door and walked out, this was at night in the dark, he was met by about ten men, or maybe more. They grabbed him and forced him back inside the house.

"Manuel was in the backyard, but he heard all this noise and went inside. The wife of Pedro was already in the house, she saw her husband and these men. When my brother got inside one of the men asked who he was, and the wife was about to say that he was her son. But my brother immediately said he was a teacher. As soon as they knew that they grabbed him, they called him a "communist teacher" and they started to force my brother and Pedro out the door.

"They wanted to spread terror so the Literacy Campaign wouldn't be successful. They didn't want the farmers to read or write. But the campaign wasn't political; they taught them basic reading skills, like they would a young child. I guess these bandits just didn't want the government to be doing anything good to help the people. I can't even understand that type of thinking. They were just evil.

"So the bandits took my brother and Pedro away. I have this information from Pedro's wife Mariana. Not too far from the house, there was a lot of vegetation, so they could hide and not be seen. The bandits beat them, they tortured them before killing them. They hung them from the same tree. Mariana ran to get help and she led the local militia to her house. They searched the area and they found the two bodies."

An examination of Pedro and Manuel determined the two were severely tortured. Manuel had his testicles cut off, and doctors estimated he had more than 20 puncture wounds. There were multiple bruises covering his body and his head. The autopsy showed he was still alive when he was hung by the neck.

"I don't want to think of how he suffered, how much pain they put him through before he died. They were really hard on him. At the funeral we saw the body and found out what had happened. My parents were destroyed. He was their only son, my father was affected so much, he felt so much responsibility for sending his son there. He never recovered."

The funeral for Manuel was attended by thousands.

"They did catch the bandits, they were tried and executed. It was not exactly what I wanted, there was no relief, but it was something. In December 1961 the Literacy Campaign ended. There were other teachers killed, I don't know how many, but there were others." (In total 14 teachers were murdered during the campaign.)

"My brother and I were very close, any problems I had I'd go to him. I think of my brother often, even to this day. You never can forget something like this. I now have one son, Norbiel, 30. My husband died many years ago. All the services and ceremonies to honor my brother, my son accompanies me. He knows the story and the details. It is important to remember. In Trinidad and Escambray every year there is a ceremony, and I try to attend. But I'm getting older and it's harder to go."

Despite the sorrow she has lived with, Maria takes some consolation in the realization her brother's efforts have not been forgotten.

"There is a school in every province in Cuba that is named after my brother. These schools graduate teachers. I feel satisfied that I see that he's remembered in that way. I'm happy to know these students have graduated from a school that honors my brother, and that they know his story."

9

Cine Móvil

The program to bring cinematic entertainment to the rural areas of Cuba was known as Cine Móvil (mobile cinema). Developed in the first year of the revolution, put into practice by 1961, Cine Móvil involved showing mostly American and Mexican popular films—comedies, dramas, action—in makeshift outdoor theaters. The films were transported on specially made trucks that also served as the projection platform.

Cine Móvil was the target of numerous attacks in the Matanzas province east of Havana from November 1962 to January 1963.

JESÚS SÁNCHEZ PÉREZ

Jesús Sánchez Pérez is a thin, well groomed man whose physical appearance is a contradiction to his 71 years. He keeps himself in good shape, "I eat healthy and I try to exercise as much as possible." Jesús speaks fluidly in clipped tones with few pauses. He lives in a comfortable apartment in Havana. Jesús is the founder of Cine Móvil and its permanent information officer.

"Before the revolution, in the remote countryside no-one watched any films. The movies were a privilege for those who lived in the cities, with the big theaters, air conditioning, the best American films were shown. The cities in Cuba showed the popular 35mm films—but nobody in the country saw any film, before the revolution, nobody.

"The Cuban Institute of Arts and Cinematography was founded in March 1959, two months after the revolution. So the will was there to take all these films to the countryside. We had so many people who later asked us if these films were Russian—no," he makes the point forcefully, almost shouting. "This was developed well before the Soviets came to Cuba. So these were not political films, we showed Charlie Chaplin, Orson Welles, Italian and Spanish and Mexican commercial films. The Russians had no influence in Cuba at that time.

Jesús Sánchez Pérez

"The only possibility to bring these films to the country was to have them shown in 16mm format, so they were portable. We had some American projectors, Bell and Howell. But we were missing a lot of parts."

Other problems had to be overcome in order to bring the films to the rural parts of Cuba.

"There were a lot of things we had to solve first, we had to get trucks and that was extremely difficult, there was not one screw left in Cuba. We had to build the trucks that were capable of projecting films. We made 30 such trucks, and then we had to get the drivers, the projectionists, all the people that were needed. And we had to teach them how to run the projectors."

Once up and running the program was a huge success.

"Everywhere we went the people would welcome this as a blessing. The whole town would turn out and go to their neighbors to bring them to see the films. How do we explain to them the type of films we would show? So we brought Cuban filmmakers and they would talk about the films to the people. You can't imagine how it felt to take art, culture to these people.

"We'd stay in each place depending on the size of the town; maybe we'd be there one day, maybe one week. We would show the films in front of ten people or in front of 1,000. Most of them had never seen a film before, especially the older ones, 70 or 80 years old, had never seen anything like it."

Jesús fondly recalls some of the most natural, and humorous reactions from the first-time audiences.

"I remember one incident in Camagüey, in this region there were plantations. We were showing *Modern Times*, the Charlie Chaplin film. There is a moment in the film where a policeman is hitting Charlie Chaplin with a stick. One farmer started to attack the screen with a machete to protect Chaplin. People reacted naturally to these films, they forgot it was a film, seeing is believing and what they saw they believed.

"Santiago Álvarez was a famous Cuban filmmaker by that time, the early 1960s. In those days there were planes coming from the US bombing sugar cane fields and Álvarez made a documentary film about these incidents and we were showing it one time. A plane was flying overhead and then the film showed this plantation catching fire. One farmer went for a bucket of water to put out the fire, and then others went to get water and do the same thing. Remember, they had nothing at the time, no radio, no TV, no film, nothing."

While the locals embraced Cine Móvil, others had a far different reaction.

"These programs provoked counter-revolutionary reaction, they were focused on the same farmers living in the areas. These were Cuban-Americans infiltrating back into Cuba. They were mercenaries, Batista men. Terrorists. These bandits saw these programs as dangerous—Cine Móvil was an enemy in their eyes. I don't know why, they saw anything the government was doing to help the people as a target, they didn't want anything to succeed. There were a lot of shootings of the Cine Móvil trucks. In Matanzas province there was an attack on a truck, it was 1962 I think. Three people were killed. This area was the worst for attacks. [The three were killed over two attacks. The first happened in November 1962, when driver Lázaro González Fagundo was shot to death near the town of Jagüey Grande. Two months later in January 1963 two others were murdered, Giraldo Mora Cartón and Andrés Casulla Perera, on the farm of Carmen Hernandez.]

"These counter-revolutionists they just wanted to create chaos at any cost. To kill someone for this, for showing films, it is monstrous. They never attacked when the films were being shown, they only ambushed the trucks with only one or two people there. They were cowards. They wouldn't dare attack when the whole town was out watching, they'd be caught and torn apart. So they waited till we left the town, when there were only the few people in the truck, that's when they'd attack, kill them and destroy the truck and equipment."

IRAIDA GONZÁLEZ FAGUNDO

Iraida's brother Lázaro was killed during an ambush just outside Jagüey Grande, a small town south-east of Havana, in Matanzas province. Lázaro was the driver of a jeep as part of the Cine Móvil program. Iraida was interviewed in a local government office in Jagüey Grande, along with her older brother Israel and sister Hilda. Despite the years that have passed since the incident, all three spoke emotionally of what happened to their brother.

"I've lived here all my life," 60-year-old Iraida commented. "It was my brother who was killed—Lázaro. November 30, 1962. He was 26 years old. He was the driver of the jeep of the revolutionary organization in charge of civilian property at the municipal level here, so it was not uncommon for him to be doing that job. The local officials would make programs to put into different areas; and Cine Móvil was one of those programs. It was organized here in town, all the logistics came from Jagüey Grande."

Iraida González Fagundo

Iraida explains why Cine Móvil was so important. "There was no electricity in the countryside, this was the first time these people would have the chance to see a film. I remember that my brother talked to me about this, he was very excited. Around 6 p.m. he left, along with the others—there were one or two more people in the jeep, as well as a few in the truck. This truck had the projection equipment and the film. The town they were going to was Quemado Grande, it was about eight kilometers away from Jagüey."

She still finds it hard to believe why anyone would want to kill someone just for wanting to show films to villagers.

"There was never a problem before this, we all knew there were bandits in the area, but no one was afraid and no one really thought that anyone would be attacked for just showing some films. Remember, however, this was the same time that these terrorists were attacking students for going to the countryside to teach farmers to read and write. The Cine Móvil people didn't have any weapons with them, they never thought they'd need them, and they weren't trained in weapons either."

Iraida turns to the details of her brother's death. "When they were going to the village they were ambushed. The jeep was at the back and they were the only ones hit. The projection truck up front was not shot at all. It was dark at night and my brother didn't see a thing. There were stone fences on either side of the dirt road and the bandits hid behind the fences, jumped out, fired their guns, then ran away. The bandits were waiting for them, they knew it was the Cine Móvil group. They just wanted to create terror, to disrupt the government and make the people afraid.

"My brother went to the surgery room and he died of internal bleeding. I was 15 years old at the time. My parents told me my brother had been killed, I didn't really understand it fully because I couldn't comprehend why anyone would kill my brother just for showing some films.

"He was married at the time, the name of his wife is Ramona Lopez, and they had two children; Sonia, four and Ileana, three. She lives in Havana now, remarried. I keep in touch with her often."

Not long after the attack, government officials were able to round up the group of terrorists.

"They found the bandits, five or six of them, about 15 to 20 days later. They put them on trial here in town, and they were sentenced to death. They were part of a larger group of terrorists, Cuban-Americans. We knew a lot of them; I was outraged, one of them played with my brother when they were children. How could you do something like that? I can't imagine it."

Iraida points out that her brother is not forgotten in Jagüey Grande. "There is a school named after my brother, as well as a small marker dedicated to his memory where he was killed, it's still there, well taken care of, off the main road now. The children go there and every year we go to participate in the memorial event."

Not surprisingly, her brother's death still affects her deeply.

"Whenever I watched a movie for years after I'd think of my brother. After the attack the people living here were very afraid to go out at night, because they were afraid to be shot. Every strange noise we heard we'd be afraid of. The other two in the jeep survived the attack—Zunilda Morejón, she died a few years ago. The other one, Israel Garcia, is still alive in town here."

ISRAEL GARCIA

Israel, 71, comes into the room with a big smile and a quick handshake. He takes his seat without further ceremony, and begins speaking rapidly, his eyes and hands moving quickly in rhythm with his speech. It does not take any prompting for him to sit down and tell his story. He tells it with humor and passion, despite the tragic nature of the event.

Israel Garcia

"This happened just one month after the October missile crisis [1962]. That time it was a terrible time with bandits. Before the Bay of Pigs it wasn't so bad, but after that it was terrible. Before that the

Escambray mountains was the center for counter-revolutionaries. All these activities here in Jagüey Grande occurred after Bay of Pigs. At one time 200 to 300 meters from the town someone was killed. Before and after the Cine Móvil incident others had been killed. So we were aware of the terrorists in the area, but no one thought they'd bother Cine Móvil.

"Two or three trucks were used for the program, we'd look for small towns in the area to take the films to show. They were not political films, only cultural ones, we'd show a lot of American films like Charlie Chaplin. The farmers loved that, they'd laugh and have a great time.

"Lázaro was the driver of the jeep, I didn't know him too well. But I knew the type of person he was, he went to the Bay of Pigs to fight off the invasion. He was a good person. He drove because I didn't have a license. This happened on a Friday, on the Wednesday before we went up to the town to promote Cine Móvil coming, we'd use loudspeakers to tell the people, so I'm sure the bandits knew about this.

"We were expecting about 200 people to attend the filming. I think this was my first time at Cine Móvil, I don't remember doing it before that. There were only three or four trucks in the province of Matanzas that had these projectors set up. There was always a demand for showing these films so we had to co-ordinate when we could use them.

"I don't think the bandits wanted to attack the jeep, which we were in, but to hit the truck that had the projector. So if we hadn't gone I'm sure the truck would have been attacked. We were in the back and the truck was in the front. We left around 7:20 p.m. It was very cold that night. The town was only eight kilometers away and we were scheduled to show the film at 8 p.m. The road was narrow and dirt, so we had to go very slow to the town, around 15 to 20 kilometers an hour. There were stone fences on both side of the road, so it was easy for the gunmen to hide."

Israel then tries to explain the positions of those in the jeep. A piece of paper is produced and he starts drawing a crude layout of the jeep—showing Lázaro in the driver's seat on the left side, another man,

Aurelio in the middle and the woman Zunilda Rodriguez Morejón on the right side; and Israel on the back seat directly behind the driver. "My right arm was hit, I don't know why I wasn't killed, when I heard the bullets I moved my arm instinctively and the shot hit my arm. The bandits used a shotgun and the shot sprayed all over my arm, and that's what hit Lázaro.

"When I was hit I yelled out, 'We're being shot', and I could hear the bullets. Afterwards we were told they used a 16 gauge shotgun, but apparently they put nails in as well. They also had some rifles. When I heard the first shot Aurelio screamed out that Lázaro had been hit, and I yelled out—'Me too!'

"They shot up the jeep as well, it was badly damaged. My first thought was to get out of the jeep. Remember it was completely dark by this time, there were no lights on this little dirt road. So I tried to jump out of the jeep. But the lower part of my pants got stuck on some part of the jeep and I went head down and I fractured my arm when I hit the jeep. It was total confusion. I am trying to jump out of the jeep, then I get stuck. Lázaro had been hit bad by then, and was bleeding to death. Aurelio was screaming on the other side, I don't think he was hit."

Israel pauses and breaks out in a grin. He's been telling this part of the story with a great deal of arm waving and facial gestures. He pauses, to reflect both on the absurdity and the terror of the incident.

"I guess it sounds a little funny to describe it this way, this is the first time I've told this story in years. I had to give a description to the officials after the incident, but I've never told it since. It's funny now, I guess, but then..." He pauses, not sure how to continue the story. After a few seconds he's back to his animated self.

"So I hit the jeep with my arm trying to get out, it fractures my arm, and it tears off a part of my face. So now I'm hanging from the jeep, with my pants caught and this jeep is dragging me along the road, this goes on until my pants broke. Once my pants let go I tumble out of the jeep and roll around on the road. And the truck with the projector is ahead of us and they didn't even hear what was going on, I guess they were too far ahead. They didn't hear us or stop for us, they just keep going on to the town.

"Then there was silence, the jeep stopped. Lázaro was wounded, Aurelio I guess by this time was in the driver's seat stopping the jeep. I was a number of meters back from the jeep, lying on the road, bleeding from my arm, my face. The next thing I remember is that Zunilda was coming back to get me, she was so courageous because no one knew where the bandits were. They could have shot and killed her when she got out of the jeep to save me. She called out my name, and for sure the bandits could have heard her and shot her, and me. By this time I had crawled over to the stone wall and was hiding, keeping very quiet.

"The people in the truck arrived at the town not knowing what had happened. So Zunilda and I talked about what to do; we decided to go straight to the town to get help, but we were very worried about Lázaro. We didn't know how bad he was, but we knew he was shot and bleeding. We knew he was hurt, and we were afraid to start the jeep again because we thought the bandits would attack.

"We got into the town and immediately called for an ambulance and when they arrived, there were two ambulances that came. One was driven by Lázaro's brother Israel, but he didn't recognize Lázaro so I had to tell him 'that's your brother', I guess he was shot up so badly in the face he didn't recognize him. There was a lot of blood."

While it was too late to save Lázaro, Israel's wounds were taken care off and his arm set. Unfortunately, he's still suffering from the level of treatment received.

"There were not too many doctors at the time, so many left after the revolution. Nobody could take care of my arm, so by the next day they still hadn't operated, it was bad, very bad for that to happen. They didn't take care of it very well, they just put it in a cast without treating it properly. When they removed the cast weeks later the doctor said it was not right, they took an x-ray and it was too late to do anything, my arm should have been operated on to set it, but it wasn't. It still bothers me, that arm, whenever I lift anything. But I can't complain I guess, I could have been killed there."

So rather than complain, he'd prefer to just keep smiling. "Now when I work and get paid, I have to stretch my arm to take the money—and that hurts, but not so much as to not get the money"—he laughs out loud, pleased at his own joke. "I have to laugh, what else can you do?"

10
La Coubre

For the sheer amount of carnage, no other act of terrorism against Cuba compares to the explosions that tore apart the French vessel *La Coubre*, resulting in a casualty toll in excess of 100 dead and 300 injured. And no other act carries with it the same level of controversy as the destruction of this ship that carried 70 tons of grenades and millions of rounds of ammunition from Belgium.

La Coubre exploded in Havana Harbor on March 4, 1960. The Cuban Revolution was just over a year old and the new government was anxious to defend itself, particularly against the increased belligerency from the United States. The Bay of Pigs invasion was still a year away, although plans for the assault were well known to the Cuban military, and there had been dozens of terrorist attacks already committed in Havana and the countryside.

So there was tremendous relief when the 4,000 tonne steamship arrived, as the United States had been putting tremendous pressure on other countries not to sell arms to the Castro regime. American officials protested to the Belgians for selling these weapons and to the French for providing transportation. A few months earlier, the British had buckled under American arm-twisting and canceled a number of arms shipments to Cuba. All this was taking place more than a year before any Soviet military assistance.[1]

La Coubre's itinerary included numerous stops before arriving in Havana. Prior to its final destination the ship called on the port of Miami, where it remained for three days. It was well known within various government circles and the counter-revolutionary community what the ship was carrying. Afterwards, Cuban authorities claimed that while the ship was in Miami, terrorists had planted two bombs, set to go off 30 minutes apart. The first explosion was the weaker of the two, causing little damage. However, the blast attracted hundreds to the area to provide help, including three of the government's most important figures—Fidel Castro, Ché Guevara and Raúl Castro. The second explosion was devastating. Many thought it was an atomic bomb, as the blast blackened the skies over Havana. Fine ash fell in the harbor for days. The Old Havana district surrounding the harbor area suffered the worst damage. An estimated 90 percent of the windows in the neighborhood were blow out, and hundreds of residences were damaged. The explosion was felt up to ten kilometers away. It was the second explosion that also resulted in the majority of the casualties, including the deaths of six French crewmen.

Part of the lingering controversy over the event stems from the fact that while the Cuban government usually took extraordinary precautions when unloading a munitions vessel, this was not the case for *La Coubre*. Under normal conditions armaments were taken off the mother ship a distance from the docks, put on floating skiffs then brought to the dockyard for discharge. *La Coubre* was allowed to tie off and unload directly.

Following the incident the Cuban government conducted an extensive investigation, coming to the conclusion the blasts could not have been accidental.

Investigators interviewed hundreds of dock workers and eye witnesses, and conducted tests to demonstrate that no amount of force used on the crates during the unloading process could have caused them to explode. They even went so far as to drop the crates from

Cuban coverage of the *La Coubre* explosion

great heights to see if the grenades or armaments would detonate. They did not.

Testimony from Estanislao Figueroa del Pozo, one of the workers unloading the munitions, outlined the extensive safety measures taken when unloading a ship with such dangerous cargo and gave his opinion as to the cause.

"Experts put the charges in place in the cargo hold... There is no doubt about that. There was no time or opportunity to do that in Havana, on account of the security measures. The explosions were caused by the deliberate placing of explosive devices.

"We had handled large quantities of munitions before. Besides, those grenades had two types of safety devices, one for transportation purposes and another, which was secured during the voyage. Huge mechanical efforts would have been required to detonate one of these grenades. Also, given the way in which they had been packaged, in wooden crates, in a zinc container and inside a cardboard case, a fall or something similar could not have been accidental. Following the explosion, an order was given at the highest levels to throw these types of crates from a plane at high altitude and they did not explode. In other words, there is no possibility whatsoever of an accident during the process of unloading the ship's cargo."[2]

The only conclusion authorities could come to was that the explosions were a deliberate act. The investigation deduced that the two bombs were hidden deep on a stack of boxes loaded with hand grenades. Neither the French nor Belgium governments conducted investigations, but both stated at the time that the ship was safely loaded and there would have been a minuscule chance that the explosions would have been caused by an accident.

On the American side, reports indicated that CIA agent Colonel J.C. King as well as Miami counter-revolutionary leader Rolando Masferrer Rojas were aware of *La Coubre* and the various ports at which it would dock. Colonel King was later involved in Operation Pluto, one of a number of covert actions against Cuba implemented in 1960.[3] To this day neither the CIA nor the US State Department has declassified any documents concerning the sabotage of the French cargo boat.[4]

The following interviews were conducted at the magnificent Dulce Maria Loynaz museum in Havana. The museum is dedicated to the renowned Cuban poet who lived in the classic Spanish mansion with her upper class family. Dulce Maria died a few years after the revolution and willed the estate to the government, who turned it into a cultural center and museum.

JUAN LUÍS RODRÍGUEZ INFANTE

Juan is a heavily built man, outgoing by nature and anxious to show off his artificial leg the moment he walks into the salon. He removes the prosthesis in one easy motion, proudly propping it up beside his real right leg, a wide grin on his face. The fake appendage covers from the knee down, complete with leather shoe and a black woolen sock. It is a badge of honor for Juan, proof of his dedication and commitment to his country.

"I was the captain of a police station outside of Havana, I came to the city to do some work. I was next to Carlos Tercero Ave, near the harbor, when I heard the first explosion. I had no idea what or where it came from, but I had a feeling it was sabotage."

In the months immediately after the Triumph of the Revolution Havana was subjected to weekly bombings from counter-revolutionaries. Anyone who heard an explosion during those days would have immediately suspected terrorism.

"When I ran closer to the explosion I saw that there was this boat on fire. So I started to work with the firemen and the police, we were helping to tend to the injured. I saw a body a few feet from where I was, so I went over and touched him to see if he was OK, and that's when I noticed he had no head. It was terrible, it was something out of a battle scene. There were bodies all over the ground, limbs and arms and feet all scattered around. So much blood on the streets, and so many people screaming and crying. People were running towards the ship trying to help out. The Cuban people have no fear, if they see something that needs help, they run right to it.

"About five meters from the ship I noticed that there was a truck loaded with hand grenades. The workers were taking the arms off the ship and putting them on the truck, which they'd take away and unload, then come back and load up more. This truck was on fire. So in order to avoid more loss of life I gathered about seven or eight people to push this truck in the water.

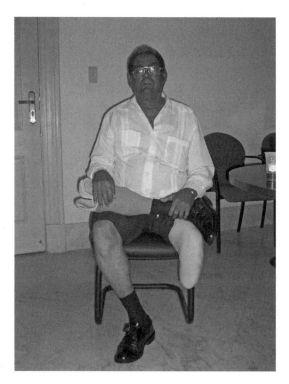

Juan Luís Rodríguez Infante

"Someone in the group refused, he thought it would be too dangerous—the truck was on fire and could have blown up at any time. So I was getting frantic and wasn't sure what to do. At that time I saw

Ché Guevara at the front, maybe 20 feet away. I ran up to Ché and I told him 'I am responsible to put the truck in the water.' He looked at me and the truck on fire and quickly pointed that the truck should be pushed in the water, he knew if it blew up it would be disastrous. You have to remember that right after the first explosion on the ship, Ché, Fidel, Raúl they all came down to the site to see if they could help. And the people were so upset, they told them all to leave because they didn't want them to be killed. But they wouldn't leave, all three were there helping. Finally we convinced them to go.

"So I rounded up the others and we went to put this truck in the water. Immediately when we started pushing there was the second explosion. This explosion killed most of the people. It was incredible. There were dozens and dozens of people without heads, arms, legs—it looked like a horror film. This second explosion was ten times bigger than the first one. It was timed to go off to cause the most destruction.

"At first I thought it was an atomic bomb, it scared the life out of me. The second explosion hit, and then I see this big mass of debris coming down, right at me. When I saw that I dove under the truck, yes, the same one that was on fire. So I went under the truck, the others were either killed or got out of the way in time. I was under the truck and the blast took my leg off, right under the knee. I felt something, it wasn't a great pain, but I felt something.

"A big piece of steel tore off my left leg from the knee down. I was always conscious—I knew I was missing my leg, I could feel my leg was gone. It wasn't long before they got me and took me to the hospital. At the hospital there were dozens of others who had been injured in the explosion. The hospital was going crazy with all these people. The next day I was happy to find out that one of my friends survived, he told me that the truck was finally pushed into the water. They had saved the armaments and recovered the truck.

"The explosion broke all the glass in the windows in Old Havana, this was the second explosion, it was about a half hour between explosions. So these terrorists knew the first explosion would attract more people, and that the second one would cause the most damage. I spent one month in hospital, after that I went back to work. It didn't take too long to get used to the artificial leg and now it's a part of me, I've had it for almost 50 years. The explosion also affected my ear and eye, my right eye is very bad and I lost hearing in the one ear."

Juan Luís remembers vividly the type of day it was on March 4, 1960.

"It was a nice day, a winter day. Very cool and sunny. After the explosion the sky darkened, there was so much ash and fire in the air. The first explosion was at 3:15 p.m. The second explosion, the worse one, was around 3:45 p.m.

"This explosion of *La Coubre*, I have never in my life seen so much damage, but still the people came to help. I feel sorry for the Cuban dead, but also for the French and the Spanish people who were killed. I have felt fear more than once in my life, but when you have to face it you become morally stronger. But I wouldn't want anyone to go through what I did that day."

ROSARIO OLEGARIO VELASCO GOMEZ

When requested to spell her full name, Rosario responds in haltering English. Asked if she understands the language, she replies coolly, "Yes, but I refuse to speak it because I hate the Americans for what they did." She says it with an angry stare that augments the impression she gives of strength and formality. Rosario is reminded that not all English speaking people are Americans, and not all Americans are similar. She smiles, somewhat condescendingly, and says in Spanish "Yo no voy a hablar English"—I'm not going to speak English.

Rosario's gruff exterior is a façade, however, betrayed throughout the interview by the overwhelming emotions these memories still invoke deep within her.

"My husband was killed at *La Coubre*. My husband's father and brother also worked at the shipyards. His brother Miguel was working in the other section of the harbor, and he started looking for my husband after the first blast," 77-year-old Rosario says.

"My husband was 33 years old when the ship exploded. Of course it was an act of terrorism, there is no doubt. His name was Arturo Garcia Vargas, but he had a nickname Manduley. At 3 p.m. he always came home to have lunch. But that day, March 4, 1960 he told me he wouldn't be coming home at that time because he'd have to work all day helping to unload this special ship.

Rosario Olegario Velasco Gomez

"We were preparing to go out on my birthday on March 6 and I was at the beauty salon when I heard the explosion, it was about ten kilometers away but I felt it. When I heard the first explosion I left to go to my house because I had a little child, I had to make sure all was fine. On the street I heard people say the explosion is at the harbor, people were yelling, it was crazy. I got into a taxi and the driver said the bomb was at a power plant, or a building. I told him if it's in the harbor go there because my husband is there.

"I think I was almost inside the area when I heard the second explosion, so many people were going to the area to help. Ambulances started to pick up the injured, taking them to all the local hospitals. I saw some injured, but I was looking for my husband.

"By chance a fellow worker of my husband met me and said maybe he's OK. I always had hope, you always do, but when I finally got there to see it, I started to think there was no hope. I called home and thought maybe there was some news. But there was nothing, so I went to a local hospital and I knew someone there—she knew something but she couldn't say anything. She said I should go home. I called again and my mother was there and she wanted me to come home—they knew he was dead. But my mother couldn't tell me over the phone. So then I went home and was told he was killed. It hit me like a rock, I was numb."

Rosario then describes the even greater shock she received when the family arrived at the hospital, expecting to have to identify her husband's body.

"We all went to the hospital—and that's when we found out that he wasn't dead. He was there in the hospital, barely alive. He was burned totally, his whole body was burned. When I first saw him I said that's not him. He was covered in bandages, head to foot. But when he heard my voice, he moved a bit, just a little bit, to my direction and I realized it was my husband. It was too painful to see him like that, it was…" Her strength and demeanor have left her as she starts to weep deeply. "I couldn't stand seeing him like that, knowing how much pain he was in, I felt dizzy, I fainted. It was too much emotion, I had prepared myself to see his body at the hospital, then to find out he was alive, then to see him in that condition, totally wrapped in bandages and burnt from head to toe, to imagine the pain he was going through. It was too much."

She stops for a moment to collect herself, trying to control her tears. The others in the room are also sobbing.

"When I recovered from the faint, I went close to him and I told him it would be ok—I will never forget this—I told him he'd recover. I know I did not believe it, but I had to tell him that. The hospital gave him superb attention, whatever he needed they took care of him. I stayed by his side constantly, for those nine days he was there. He survived in that condition for nine days, can you imagine that?

"After a few days he started to speak a bit, he told me that he had been working at the warehouse when the first explosion took place. He spoke slowly, softly, but I think he knew I was with him and he wanted to tell me what happened. At the end he couldn't speak much, only to look at me. I'd talk to him but he didn't respond much. The last day, he hadn't spoken for two or three days before, but that last day he asked about our son. He was four years old then, Miguel Ángel. I didn't want to bring him to see his father, because he was in such bad shape.

"Every day after the explosion, when my husband was in the hospital, and afterwards, I was told that my son would start running around the house, at around 5 p.m. This was the same time his father would come home. He was very close to his father, and later when I told this to a psychiatrist he explained it was just a way for the boy to deal with what had happened. He knew his father was sick, but we didn't tell him everything, he was so young he wouldn't have understood.

"My husband, all he said was that he wanted to see his son. It was his last wish. So I decided to bring our son to the hospital. We took him into the room and when he saw his father he didn't want to accept it. My son had this terrible, twisted expression on his face. Immediately he started screaming, 'What happened to my father?' No one in the hospital room said anything, it was terrible. You can never forget something like that.

"When he passed away the doctors removed the bandages and dressed him. They showed me the x-rays, it was awful to see him. When they removed the bandages his back was filled with metal particles and he was burned all over. There were holes all over his back from where these small pieces of metal buried into him from the explosion. I don't know how he survived those nine days, the pain he was suffering no one could survive it. His whole body was impacted. His back was like a cheese grater, he had all the holes."

Rosario can no longer continue with the description. Instead, she turns to the type of man her husband was.

"He was a humble person. Baseball was his favorite sport. I met him at the Havana carnival. My family didn't like him at first, that's the way it always is, maybe because I was young, I was a student and he was a worker. But afterwards, my family accepted and loved him. We were married eight years, and we only had the one son. I've never remarried.

"All these years have passed but it is still so hard for me to talk about it. No one had the right to kill this person. He was doing an honest day's work to help the Cuban people.

"I was waiting for my birthday party, to go to a dance—instead I had to go to the hospital and watch and wait for him to die."

ALBERTO SOLIS SOTOLONGO

The 63-year-old Alberto is the type of Cuban you can readily find across the country; one who speaks consistently in a strong voice, whether giving directions to the local *mercado* or arguing with passion on the subject that concerns most everyone—baseball. During the interview his tone dominates. Even when interviewed alone his voice rises in anger when recalling the smallest details.

Alberto is the coordinator of the organization for victims of *La Coubre*, an appropriate choice as he is obsessed with all aspects of the event. He is the acknowledged expert on all things regarding the ship. And he is not shy to share his opinions.

"My father was killed at *La Coubre*, his name was Alonso Solis Viarica. He was 53 years old. He was a dock man, taking cargo off the boat and putting it on the trucks. He worked at the docks for ten years. This boat, *La Coubre*, was filled with ammunition. Normally they would take the ammunition off the main boat and put it on smaller skiffs to bring it to the harbor. This time, with *La Coubre*, they were unloading it directly at the docks. I don't know why they did that. I think they wanted to get it off as soon as possible, there was a lot of tension regarding military things in those days. Lots of terrorist activity in the city.

"It was a very difficult time because the United States was pressuring countries not to sell arms to Cuba, the United States did not want the Cuban government to have any means to defend itself. This was just a few months after the revolution and already there was this force against us.

Alberto Solis Sotolongo

"How do I know it was sabotage? The security of the ship, the customs offices, they all had guarantees and assurances that it was impossible for any element of the ship to explode. They knew what this ship was carrying and they made special efforts to ensure it was safe to transport. The Cuban government tested the ammunition afterwards, and they showed the munitions could not explode on their own, that it was no accident. There was no mechanical malfunction of the ship.

"It was shown that there was a box on board, there was a device that when it was lifted it produced the explosion. The box was put on a stack of grenades. These explosions were timed to go off 30 minutes from one another.

"There was a complete investigation. This ship made several stops, and the last one was in Miami. It stayed in Miami for a few days and it would be very easy for someone to come onboard and plant those bombs."

Alberto turns his memory to the day of the explosion. "I was at home at 3 in the afternoon and I felt the first blast. I lived in Havana not close to the harbor but when I heard the explosion I ran to the area. I wasn't allowed to pass. There were police and military there and they weren't allowing anyone to go through. Then a short while later there was the second explosion. I was maybe 100 meters from the ship.

"I saw people running away, they were screaming and crying, some were bleeding, I went to look for my father, I knew he was working on the docks that day. I didn't know where my father was, I went from hospital to hospital looking, the hospitals were being filled up with the injured people, it was hard to get anyone to talk to you.

"I went to the coroner's office, but I don't want to remember—there were all these containers of bodies—no heads, no arms or legs, bodies burnt by the flames, and no one able to identify them. It seemed they had never recovered the body of my father, several times I opened the boxes that contained the bodies of the dead. On the third day I found a survivor who worked with my father. He told me that my father could be found in box drawer number 85.

"The body was so badly damaged I couldn't, I couldn't tell who it was. I asked for fingerprints. This body had lost its face, arms, and was burnt completely. But then, I looked closer and I saw the clothes of my father. It was very, very hard to accept that, to look at this burnt mess and know it was my father.

"I was 15 years old, the government took care of all the families, and they are still taking care of us. But I also had to look after my family, I was the man of the house now and I was still just a kid. My mother had to go to start working at that time but later she had to quit, she got sick and never recovered. It was very different after that, I had to work; I worked in a mechanical shop, worked in different factories. I became a leader of a trade association, I'm still working with the national syndicate of tradesmen. I'm also the co-ordinator of *La Coubre* victims group; we organize meetings and other events. The organization takes in all aspects of acts of terrorism. What happened to us all, we remember all the time, but *La Coubre* is the most criminal act, more criminal than the Cubana Airlines bombing, because there is total silence about this, the truth has been hidden but there is so much proof that this was an act of terrorism."

11
Department Stores

From December 1960 to April 1961, a number of famous department stores in Havana were the targets of terrorist bombings.

La Época, El Encanto, Flogar and even the American Woolworth (known as the 10 Cents store) were damaged in this series of attacks. The stores were all located on Havana's most famous commercial street, Av de Italia, known more familiarly as Galiano.

The worst incident was the fire at El Encanto on April 13, 1961 which completely destroyed the landmark edifice. Of all the department stores, El Encanto was considered to be the finest, offering exclusive lines in clothes and attracting the majority of high end shoppers. The damage was so great that it was decided to tear down the remains of this magnificent eight-story building that was home to hundreds of employees. With the building leveled, a park was developed in its place, which remains to this day. Those visiting the area can still find the small plaque in honor of the store and the one person who died in the bombing—Fe del Valle—who lost her life trying to recover a large sum of donated money that was earmarked for a local school.

The firebombing of El Encanto took place just prior to the Bay of Pigs. Evidence showed that sticks of dynamite were brought into the store stuffed into stockroom dolls. The series of bombs and acts of terror in this time period was designed to instill confusion among the population leading up to the invasion by the exile force, supported

Plaque commemorating the death of Fe del Valle, killed in the El Encanto explosion

by the American government. Antonio Veciana, a CIA agent accused of planning the bombing at the store, was head of Alpha 66 at the time. Other evidence pointed to the People's Revolutionary Movement (MRP), a counter-revolutionary group operating in Havana, as the ones responsible.[1]

One of the few former employees still around from that day is Luis José Campa Sánchez.

LUIS JOSÉ CAMPA SÁNCHEZ

The 72-year-old Luis José Campa Sánchez lives a quiet life in the October 10 neighborhood of Havana. Luis speaks in short, clipped sentences, his eyes and hands animated. He brings with him some faded yellow copies of the newspapers and magazines that reported on the destruction of the store. He also has in his possession photos of El Encanto when it was the highlight of the city's most important commercial avenue.

Luis José Campa Sánchez

"El Encanto—it was one of the largest department stores in Havana, along Galiano. El Encanto was a large store, eight floors, and it stocked everything, from clothes to furniture to kitchen items to anything else you wanted. I think it was the biggest, and best on the street. There were other department stores along with El Encanto; La Época and the 10 Cents were the others close by on the same street. All three were subject to terrorist attacks, but only El Encanto was destroyed completely.

"I was a clerk at El Encanto department store. I entered as a sales boy in the store, it was in 1953. I was 18 years old at the time. I worked in the store before and after the revolution. There was not a lot of difference, the pay was about the same, so were the working conditions. The store was nationalized in 1961, less than two years after the revolution."

Luis reveals that at the time of the explosion he wasn't even supposed to be at the store.

"I was off work for a few days, taking a break, but I remember I was in the vicinity of the store so I thought I'd just go in and visit some colleagues. There was also a meeting going on there at the same time, so I thought I'd go. Afterwards I wanted to talk to another manager, so I stayed. Just by coincidence I was there.

"The fire took place April 13, 1961. This was two days before the Bay of Pigs invasion, and there were lots of acts of terrorism before the invasion. La Época was bombed before the invasion, it was a terrible time. All sorts of bombs were going off before the Bay of Pigs. There was a wave of terrorism. Everyone was scared to go out.

"At every store there were a number of workers watching, because they all knew there was this possibility of bombs, we tried to be ready. The day of the fire, I remember I was on the third or fourth floor, and the phone rang. I picked it up and someone on the other end asked me, "Is the store on fire?" I said no, there was no fire here. I thought it was such a strange call. I can still remember that call so well, I can remember the voice. That phone call? I have no idea, I don't want to speculate.

"Anyway, this stayed in my mind and I told a friend. Where was I? Maybe I was on the first floor, I'm sure of that now. So I told my friend about this phone call, and we went to the fifth floor and as soon as we got there we saw smoke. We started to warn the other workers about this sabotage. We got back down to the first floor and called the firemen, when they came I went back to the other floors to see if there was anyone else in the store. This was around 6 or 7 p.m. and the store was closed, there were no customers, just workers.

"The smoke was very bad by then, it was dense, it was suffocating me and the others. I tried to make my way through but it was hard to see anything, no one knew if there were people trapped or what was going on. It only took a few minutes for the fire to spread from floor to floor. The firemen were there trying to contain the fire, but by then it was out of control, the whole building was completely covered in fire.

"There was one woman—Fe del Valle—she was able to get out but then went back to the upper floors, she remembered there was some money in a vault upstairs that belonged to a school. The store was doing some fundraising for this school and the money that was being collected was kept there in that vault, the event was sponsored by the women's organization at the store. Fe was part of that organization. She died trying to get that money, she didn't make it out and they found her body two or three days later. It was an incredibly courageous thing for her to do, she was only concerned for the school and the money that had been raised for it. El Encanto was completely destroyed, they never put another store in its place. Now there's a park with a plaque and a little statue in memory of Fe del Valle."

Luis switches the conversation to the culprit, and reveals that it was a fellow worker who set the fire.

"He belonged to a counter-revolutionary group, these people were setting bombs and doing all sorts of things, to create confusion and terror in Havana. The person who set the fire was caught and admitted he did it, explained how he set the packages to catch fire, I remember he said he hid one in a child's toy. His name was Carlos González."

With the store completely destroyed, the workers had to look for new work.

"Afterwards, the government guaranteed jobs for those who worked at the store, nobody lost their job because of that act of terrorism."

12
Pinar Del Rio Theater

The city of Pinar Del Rio is known as the capital of Cuba's best tobacco growing province. With a population of just over 150,000 it has all the traditional aspects of a Cuban town—narrow streets, concrete homes, the ubiquitous apartment blocks, a variety of hospitals, medical facilities and sports arenas. During the Special Period of the early 1990s it was known as having more bicycles per capita than anywhere else in Cuba.

One of the main cultural centers in the city during the 1950s and 60s revolved around the large Cine Riego theater, which specialized in showing Hollywood movies and cartoons on Saturday afternoons. The tradition continued following the revolution. Even after the theater was nationalized and renamed by the Cuban government the American commercial films were still being shown to the delighted audiences.

Unfortunately, the theater was also the center of one of the most horrific acts of terrorism in Cuba, on May 28, 1961.

Survivor Facundo Naranjo Delgado describes the afternoon of horror.

FACUNDO NARANJO DELGADO

"It was a Sunday, May 28, 1961 at the Cine Riego which was named after the owner of the theater—there were a chain of *cines* and pharmacies owned by this man, before the revolution. The cinema was located on Marti Street, near the city's main commercial area. It's still there now but it was renamed Pedro Zaidén theater. This was the best theater in Pinar. But that day, it was the worst place to be.

"I was 13 years old when it happened, this day there was a holiday in Pinar, a celebration of some sort, so there was a special matinee, two films and one short cartoon. I don't remember the film, but I do remember the cartoon.

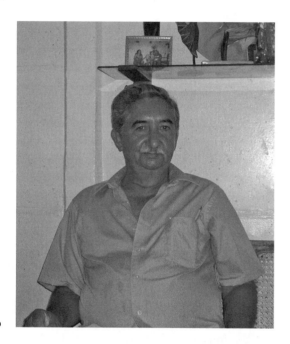

Facundo Naranjo Delgado

"It was a big place, about 400 children and parents were there, it was filled. The smallest kids would go with their adults, but we were too old for that. The first feature film started around 9 or 10 a.m.—it was still a private movie theater then so they'd have fixed times to go and you had to be there early if you wanted to get in, and get a good seat. In 1967 they nationalized the theater when the owner left.

"During the intermission they'd show the cartoon, and I liked that the best. For about an hour they'd show cartoons. This one cartoon I'll never forget, because of what happened that day. It was a Pinocchio cartoon, he was having an ice cream cone, and then the cone would catch on fire.

"There was a group of people against the revolution, and I guess they thought this would be one way to get revenge after the Bay of Pigs [April 1961]. So this group got into the theater before the show and put a bunch of phosphorous, they put it below the screen. The curtains were made of a special, heavy fabric. These guys knew the cartoon, they'd show it regularly. They knew at the moment that Pinocchio had the ice cream cone that was on fire, Pinocchio would throw the cone on the floor, and they timed the bomb to go off at that exact moment. Immediately the curtain caught fire, then it spread in just a few seconds to the first few rows of the theater and the big fans on the ceiling helped spread the fire.

"I was in row 24. There was confusion, and I got out of the seat and started to run. The first groups rushed to the doors to get out and away from the fire. There was so much screaming, the little kids were yelling for their parents and everyone else was shouting. And the theater started to fill with smoke. The only exits were at the front and everyone was crushing to get to them. But there was something blocking, no one was leaving the theater, they couldn't get the doors open, which made everyone scream and yell more. People were being knocked down and stepped on, and children were being separated from their parents.

"We found out later that when the doors were closed to show the film, these guys grabbed some iron bars and slid them through the outside door handles so they wouldn't open from the inside. They wanted everyone to die in that theater.

"It came out later that the doorman was part of this and he helped put the iron bars on the doors so the people couldn't get out. What type of person do you have to be to do that?"

The toll from the bombing was substantial. "There were 26 children hurt, six very young. Fourteen adults were also injured, a few seriously.

There were so many who were harmed by the smoke, and suffered small cuts and bruises. Fortunately no one died, I don't know how, there was so much panic, people pushing and shoving and falling over each other. It was a miracle that there were no deaths."

The miracle came in the form of a marching band.

"This was a holiday in Pinar Del Rio, and by chance there was a parade of military men, who happened to be going by just at the same time. They saw the theater was on fire and they ran there and were able to open the doors. If not... If the military parade hadn't passed by and helped release the doors, hundreds would have died."

Facundo didn't escape unharmed, although he considers that very much a part of the miracle.

"I was hurt, I got knocked down scrambling to get out and people were running over me in panic, I was knocked unconscious. I ended up with a broken arm. I was taken to the hospital, unconscious, I don't remember much about when I got hit. I spent 40 days in hospital, the break was very bad, I had injuries to my head."

Facundo admits that it was a long time until he was able to go to a theater again. "It was 1974 the next time I went to the *cine*, many years passed. Every time I passed by the theater I felt a reaction. I went to other cinemas but still had this fear. And my parents were afraid any time I'd go. I still think of it all the time, I have nightmares of that day still, nightmares of people running to the doors and not being able to get out."

13

The Cuban National Identity

El vino, de platano, y si sale agrio, es nuestro vino.
The wine, from banana, if it is sour, is our wine.
José Marti

The Cuban national identity, particularly since the Triumph of the Revolution, has been intensely defined by José Marti's declaration of the country's determination to forge its own destiny—imperfections and all. Marti, one of Cuba's most important national figures, spoke those words during the 1898 Second War of Independence. After hundreds of years of Spanish colonialism, a half century of American hegemony, the Cubans in 1959 were finally able to wrest control of their land for their national interests, not for those of a foreign power. The revolution was and remains home grown, and continues to be the well of strength the government draws from to maintain sustenance. It is a fact that has consistently escaped the recognition, intentional or not, of the regime's opponents.

The Cuban national identity is characterized by a number of elements—friendly, community spirited, a strong sense of humor mixed with oft time critical self-depreciation, a sense of assurance bordering on arrogance. In totality, these parts derive from the overarching character—the desire for independence and making something of their country from their own efforts. Accepting the mistakes, overcoming the struggles and working towards what is hoped to be a better society. And above all, the sense it is all uniquely Cuban.

Fidel Castro's Revolution in 1959 provided the opportunity to put Marti's words into practice. Through massive economic and political change, isolation, compromise, forced limitations and unrelenting aggression from the United States, the Cuban national identity has been increasingly characterized by the defiance of whatever shortcomings there may be in life, nothing is more significant than self-determination.

Defiance has been a critical element in defining what it is to be Cuban since the revolution. The call for resistance against the American imposed siege was articulated by Fidel Castro when he spoke of then President Bush's plan to increase restrictions in 2004—"our people will stand up to your economic measures, whatever they may be. Forty-five years of heroic struggle against the blockade and economic war against threats, aggressions, plots to assassinate its leaders, sabotage and terrorism have not weakened but rather strengthened the revolution."[1]

For those who have stayed and continue to support the revolution, the perspective of defiance through self-determination continues to be paramount. And while the Cuban personality is a jumble of characteristics and contradictions (as are most national identities) the cement that holds it together is the pride in autonomy—as Lesme Jardines of Havana once said in a twist on Marti and Shakespeare—"even if our rose doesn't smell as sweet, it is our rose."

The war against terrorism and American aggression has greatly tested the strength of what it is to be Cuban. The island's society, culture and people have been altered as a result of the compromises demanded from 50 years of hostility and the hundreds of acts of terrorism. The resultant siege mentality and unconditional demand for *patria* (unity) has driven the government into implementing security policies that have curtailed certain civil rights, nurtured an individual culture of suspicion complete with a language of political code, and has cultivated a sense of fatalism and black humor that marks much of the modern identity.

While terrorism has never been the dominant factor influencing Cuban society, it has played an important part in forging the national identity.

EMILIO COMAS

Emilio Comas is a poet, author and editor. He was a contributor to *Scars in the Memory*, a Cuban compilation on the subject of terrorism. Born in Caibarién, Emilio knew many of the fishermen kidnapped and tortured in the 1970s.

He spoke of the historical aggression of the United States towards Cuba and the social costs.

Emilio Comas

"American aggression against Cuba did not start at the revolution. The United States has wanted Cuba long before that, dating back to the 1820s. America has never supported Cuban independence. There are many examples throughout history, they never let us breathe with our own lungs. The revolution of 1933 is just one example.[2] We could have had a different society if not for US aggression. We've been compelled to take certain measures to protect ourselves, some catastrophic, because of the pressures from America.

"We have one of the best armies in Latin America, and we are a poor and small country. There is tremendous cost to maintain the army, and some of the best people went into the military. Cuba has one of the best intelligence services, and that costs millions to maintain—if we had normal relations with the United States we could have used those resources, those people, to better our society. We could have put more resources in products, to increase the material needs to make life easier for everyone."

While material limitations have been a fact of life within the revolution, Cuban culture has flourished, he says.

"José Marti said, 'In order to be free you have to have culture.' One of the greatest things the revolution did was to provide everyone with the possibility of accessing culture and education. I have five children. My parents were humble, poor, uneducated. Thanks to the revolution I'm an intellectual today and all my children are university graduates. Education has to be the underlining of liberty, human rights, but people also need food, housing, medicine in order to develop a cultural society. The revolution has given us the basic human needs, and helped advance culture and society. But it has not been easy, under the terrorism, the blockade."

Like many in Cuba, Emilio is aware of what the opponents say. "The Cuban government is criticized for many things, civil rights, press restrictions, treatment of dissidents. But try and imagine a person on the floor and he has a boot on his neck and you ask him to smile. They can not ask the Cuban government to provide full political civil liberties under these conditions of aggression, of all the years of terrorism, with these Cuban-American groups in Miami still plotting. Security of the nation is more important.

"Once the terrorism and the blockade ends, then we can breathe and find out what we want from our society. Americans and the dissidents confuse concepts of liberty and concepts of democracy regarding human rights. What government would allow a demonstration that has been supported by a foreign government, one that publicly says it wants to overthrow our system? Would the United States allow an opposition movement inside the US that was financed and supported by Al Qaeda?

"You can't permit this under the history of terrorism and aggression we've gone through. That does not mean the revolution doesn't have defects, we've screwed up things for sure, but let us find our own way without the threat of terrorism and the economic blockade."

Cuban society has also been under enormous stress since the Special Period following the fall of the Soviet Union, when more than 40 percent of GDP was lost between 1990 and 1994.

"After the Special Period there has been a decline of some of our values. The revolution was based on the needs of the community being more important than individual needs, and that is being challenged in some ways now. One aspect of that is a part of society has accepted foreign money, and is finding another way of living. Some of these people are dangerous because our system has to be based on support and unity and there are certain ideological aspects being manifested now that are having a negative effect on society, creating divisions between those who have access to foreign money and those that do not. Our unity and community are being tested."

Emilio describes the typical Cuban as "friendly, sincere, spontaneous, generous. What happens to my neighbor is my problem; our sense of community extends beyond the immediate family, further than most cultures. And that is a product of the level of education we have; *hasta las prostitutas*" (even the prostitutes).

The flip side of that personality is, "We are very heroic but not stable, people will go out to help in hurricanes without question, then complain when the government doesn't resolve things immediately. Cubans like to complain about everything and they expect everything, but I think that's the fault of the system here, it's very paternalistic. People who see the defects of socialism don't have any reference, so they blame socialism but they don't understand what they have here compared to other developing countries. They try and compare us to the United States and that's impossible. For me, all I want is for our country to be able to show America what we can do in peace."

HAYMEL ESPINOSA GÓMEZ

Brotherhood is the dominant Cuban trait, says Haymel Espinosa, daughter of Cubana Airlines co-pilot Miguel.

"After my father died in the Cubana Airlines bombing in 1976, we had so many people come over, not only friends but people we never knew, come by and share our suffering. It gave me and my mother so much support, strength to carry on.

"We have a spirit of brotherhood in this country. Something that upsets the Cuban people or hurt us, we respond. This happens naturally, this is part of us. Who does not have a friend, a brother a relative that has not been affected by terrorism? It helps us all overcome these tragedies."

She feels this brotherhood comes from a sense of justice, heightened as a result of the war against terrorism.

"The Cuban people have long been attacked, and we have learned how to defend ourselves. Anything that we thought was done unfairly to us, we want to reclaim it. We demonstrate with marches in front of the United States interest section. In the 1970s when the fishermen were captured. I remember going to the street to protest these acts. Then I'd march along the same street to defend my cause.

"Terrorism has also forced us to organize. We've had to create forms to defend our country. Cubans are active politically, for good or bad. The best thing to be is organized. We can mobilize in a short period of time. Groups like the Cuban Women's Federation, the Young Pioneers, UJC [Union of Cuban Youth], CDR [Committee for the Defense of the Revolution] these are the groups of the masses, and transcends the political."[3]

For Haymel, the typical Cuban is someone who is, "Happy, educated, cultured, nationalistic and very sensitive. Wherever a Cuban is needed, in a party or in a funeral, we'll be there. We are quick to defend our just cause and defend the cause of any Cuban. But we can be very forgiving, we are strong that way. I think the best characteristics of Cubans have surfaced at the most difficult moments. Look at what happened during the hurricanes last year,[4] those with the strongest homes invited their neighbors to stay with them. Everyone helped each other."

Haymel expresses a theme consistent with many Cubans who continue to support the revolution, and a perspective that seems to baffle those on the other side of the Florida Straits. Despite the difficulties and limitations, there is no thought of overthrowing the current regime.

"A Cuban who has dignity can't think of revolting against this government. We have always fought for community; we have learned our struggles were for good education, food, for the children, for health. Those were our reasons for struggling, and we continue."

Haymel shakes a stern finger at the American politicians and the counter-revolutionaries who don't understand. "There is liberty here, democracy, we don't tell lies, our judicial system is fair—not like what has happened to the Cuban Five. There is so much propaganda from the Americans who shout that they want to bring liberty to Cuba. We have liberty here, our liberty. We have our society created by us, it is different but it is ours."

RAMÓN TORREIRA

If José Marti is generally considered to be one of the most influential figures in the fight for Cuban independence, the man who should be recognized as the father of the country's national identity is Félix Varela Morales.

That's the opinion of Ramón Torreira, an expert on Operation Peter Pan as well as an investigator at CIPS, the Center for Sociological and Psychological Investigations in Havana. He remarks that Varela, a representative of the Spanish Cardinal in the 1820s, had a vital influence on the emerging sense of Cuban nationalism.

"This was under Spanish colonial rule, and Félix Varela recognized that it was important to work towards Cuban independence. He was first a reformist, then an ardent nationalist. He was the first professor of constitutional rights of Cuba. He had a tremendous influence on Cuban nationalism; a generation later José Marti was greatly inspired by Félix Varela."

During American hegemony from 1898 to 1959 few Cuban history books mentioned Varela; teaching Cuban children about the father of Cuban nationalism was considered dangerous, Ramón asserts. That was one of the main reasons why the government had to reform education after the revolution, to address those historical wrongs. "To have Cuban history written by Cubans, not by foreigners."

Today the highest honor bestowed by the Cuban Ministry of Culture is called the Félix Varela Morales award.

Ramón agrees that the Cuban national identity today is highly linked by the constant aggression by the United States, including the war against terrorism.

"Our awareness of working together and accepting sacrifice has been increased because of what we have had to overcome. This aggression has accelerated the process of social and political radicalism in Cuba. The Cuban Revolution was the end result of the long history of hostility by the American government, it is a historical process that started long before the revolution. Which country consistently frustrated Cuban independence? It was the United States.[5] And they continue to punish Cuba for its independence."

The result, Ramón points out, is a heightened appreciation of being Cuban.

"The impact of American aggression has been to help drive the Cuban national identity and sense of independence. There are of course many factions, but I am sure it's the one that has played an important role in the community of our people. In our defense of social rights, our desire for sovereignty.

"I feel very proud to be part of the Cuban people, we have achieved a social appreciation above individualism, which does not deny the contradictions that are generated because of the changes the revolution brought. And there is a daily consciousness and a social consciousness in this context.

"Here's an example. In my case, I feel very uncomfortable because I want to have some good coffee to serve, but I don't have any, I can't afford it or there just isn't any. I complain a lot but I can live without coffee. The stability of the government, the safety of the country, the fight against terrorism, that's more important. But I'm human, of course I'm going to complain. Let's take transportation, you stand at the bus stop and you listen to others complain. We Cubans live to complain, we do it very well. But come January 1, July 26 [national holidays] if there is no transportation the people go on foot and no one complains. They go because they want to, not because they are obligated to. The bus stop is the daily conscience, it is a way to release pressure, but going to the Revolutionary Square is an act of social conscience, we are aware of the message we want to send to the rest of the world, it is a message of support. Americans don't understand that. They don't understand our mentality so they think everyone wants the American way of life.

"Let's talk about human rights, something the government is criticized for. The international community has to re-evaluate what real human rights are. And define when a human right is violated and why. The right to education, to medicine, to food and to housing. Those are human rights. Does every country have those rights? No. But Cuba does. We complain about all the daily limitations connected to those rights, but we have those rights.

"The Cuban government had to take measures to secure the population under this aggression and terrorism, and Cuba is criticized for some of those policies. But what right does one government have to tell another what to do, what right do they have to tell another country what leaders it should have, what right do they have to tell another country what social, political and economic system they should have? And what right do they have to conduct such aggression, such terrorism, against that country? What should a country do to protect itself and its citizens?

"I don't feel oppressed or controlled by my government. There were steps that had to be taken for security, to protect the people against this aggression. Those are civil aspects, not basic human rights.

"Cuba's original sin—we have never accepted the imposition or will of imperialism, first from the Spanish and now from the Americans. We are being punished and will never be forgiven for that."

MARINA OCHOA

Cuban culture is often defined by the distress of separation. For the past 50 years families have chosen whether to stay or go, and for Cuba, this separation is not just a physical condition, but emotional and spiritual. Because few things are more precious to the Cuban national identity than family.

The aggression against the revolution that has led to so many separated families has tested the strength of the Cuban character to its core.

Marina Ochoa has had to draw extensively on that strength. She's been touched by terrorism twice: having seen her brother Frank leave under Operation Peter Pan in 1963, then almost losing her seven-year-old daughter Angela to the Dengue 2 outbreak in 1981. Marina has been part of the cultural attempt to find a level of healing and reconciliation. She has produced documentaries touching on the personal cost of separation, usually through her experience with Peter Pan.

"For the past 20 years Cuban culture has been focusing on the social and emotional consequences of family separation. In the 1980s one of the first films to explore this was on the Tony Maceo Brigade based on 55 brothers returning to Cuba for the first time since the revolution. This was the first of dozens of films that took another perspective, this time from those who left Cuba. It showed that there were victims from the other side. These were films that showed that the Cubans who stayed here were not the only victims of terrorism and aggression against our country. Particularly in the case of Peter Pan, for those children who left so young and alone, they were victims as well."

Marina suggests the various aspects of the Cuban identity have been vital in overcoming the years of aggression and terrorism.

"Terrorist activities come in many forms, as does the aggression. One type of terrorism is the physical; there is a violent reaction, it's immediate, and the natural response is anger. These acts of terrorism, they would provoke anger in any population. But it is the characteristic of the Cuban people, the anger was addressed to those responsible, to those people who carried out the acts and to the politicians who supported them. Cubans always knew where to address their anger. We never felt anger against the people of the United States, just the politicians, the government that would allow this, and those who did it. But we didn't hate the American people, or those who were not involved.

"This was a result of our culture, our ideology and the tremendous amount of information we have. That's important because when people are well informed they can act in a more rational way. The Cuban identity has always been idiosyncratic; we have very high human values, morals, ethics. All these are aspects of the revolutionary ideals, it is based on these aspects and that is what makes up the Cuban mentality.

"This *pueblo*, it is fundamentally humane by essence. The consequence of terrorism is that it agitates the whole population. A bomb has a direct immediate effect, but other aggressions against Cuba have had a deeper, longer impact. The embargo, it has worked against Cuba for so many years, it has developed in the Cuban personality a war resistance mentality—it has made them determined not to give up. It is our siege that we live with daily.

"The blockade, the terrorist acts, have all been designed to make things so bad that the Cuban people will rise up and overthrow the government. This is the justification from the other side. This is science fiction. It exists only in the minds of the American politicians and those Cuban-Americans who support these policies.

"Here is an example. President Clinton, after the Soviets collapsed, in order to achieve American policy success in Cuba he made a bit of a bluff. He allowed new policies against Cuba—Torricelli Act and Helms-Burton.[6] It was thought those would finally bring down the Cuban government. This was through the influence of the hard right Cuban-Americans. Cuba was totally vulnerable at this time, people were demoralized with the Soviet collapse and our Special Period. It was a run for you life period, where solving your own problems became more important than anything else. We were overwhelmed. The United States made this worse. Clinton could have lifted the blockade, ended the travel restrictions. What would have happened if the blockade and aggression ended? The Cuban government would have had two choices—say no to the American tourists, continue not to trade with US. The other choice would have been to accept normalization. Either way would have had an important impact on Cuba. But the American politicians don't even follow their own principles, and that is scary.

"I support the government but I also criticize, that's another propaganda myth the other side tries to promote—people criticize what is happening here and nothing happens to them. I criticize but I'm a social optimist. Once you learn those roots you never change."

ARIEL ALONSO PÉREZ

For Ariel Alonso Pérez, the two most important factors in the Cuban national identity are determination and a good sense of humor.

"Cuba has always had determination, to suffer and survive whatever is needed. During the Second Independence War of 1898 the Spanish general Valeriano Weyler put hundreds of thousands of Cubans in re-concentration camps so that the farmers couldn't provide food or help to the rebels. Thousands died in these camps, under terrible conditions. However, the Cubans continued to resist and we were winning the war against Spain. It's similar today, we are fighting an economic war, a war against terrorism—there is so much against us but we continue to struggle and fight.

"During the Dengue 2 outbreak we had to buy equipment to spray, to control the mosquitoes. When we were trying to buy this equipment the American government put pressure on countries not to sell it to us; so we had to eventually buy it from Japan, very quickly and secretly before the Americans found out. It cost us much more than if we were able to purchase this equipment from countries closer to us; but we couldn't. That's the effect of the blockade, of American aggression. And that's just one example.

"So after 50 years should we give up? *Que va!* There is an old slogan—Cuba neither gives up nor sells itself. The Cuban people are born to win and not to be beaten. This sense is still prevalent today, even in the younger generation. Of course there are great economic problems here, and many leave for those reasons, but still there is an overwhelming sense of resistance to this aggression."

Ariel is an expert on the biological war against Cuba, having studied the various plant and animal diseases the government claims to have been intentionally introduced, including Dengue 2 that killed more than 100 children. He's also a keen observer of the contradictions of the Cuban personality.

"I'll give you an example. In Santiago [Cuba's largest east coast city] CNN was doing a report on Cuba, wanting to show the discontent and problems. There was a young man with a US t-shirt talking shit about the government and another lady doing some black market selling. So they wanted to talk to these people but then it turned into a revolutionary meeting—everyone was eager to talk about the problems they were facing, but they all supported the government and no one wanted to have the Americans come back and take over. That's the way it is, but the American politicians don't understand that.

"Here's a joke to explain it better—The United States sends a group of social psychologists to Cuba to do research. They walk on the street to find out why this revolution has not been defeated, despite all the hardship. So they go back to America and meet with the president. They say it will be very difficult to defeat the revolution—the Cubans don't work but they fulfill all the plans of production; they fulfill all the plans of production but they have nothing; they have nothing but they resolve everything; they resolve everything but they are all unhappy; they are all unhappy but they all love Fidel. How do you defeat that?

"This is the contradictions of life in Cuba, of the Cuban personality. It is our conviction that we have to be free. The Americans say they want to 'free us.' Don't bother; we are free because we have our own country."

MANUEL CALVIÑO

The psychological effects of terrorism are of particular interest to one of the most respected and popular personalities on Cuban television, Manuel Calviño. For years this professor of psychology at the University of Havana has entertained millions of viewers with his energetic, disarming and engaging style. The key to his success is that he is able to speak *to* the people, not over them. Currently Calviño has a 15 minute show on Friday nights at 10 p.m. on Cuba Vision called *Vale la Pena* (Worth the effort). The show reflects on the trials and tribulations of daily life. Previously he hosted *Contacto*, a two hour show that responded directly to call-in questions.

Calviño, 57, considers the Cuban character an essential part in how the nation has been able to survive 50 years of terrorism.

"Terrorism has a direct psychological effect. Not just for the short term but middle and long term. The notion of terrorism has to do with the psychological impact, fear, and this intensity level can do plenty of damage to the person. When you say terrorism, it has a very important psychological impact. That means the person is under a condition out of himself. The person's natural behavior is being inhibited by this fear and stress. The normal movement of life is being inhibited, his projection of his future.

"The terrorist seeks to provoke the most irrational affects on a person, to unleash the most basic emotions and reactions of the person to break the normal union of the person. To alter the victim's way of life. A person is recognized as a person when he owns his own life, when he is able to react rationally. So the terrorist tries to make this person react irrationally."

Manuel Calviño

For 50 years and beyond the Cuban population has had to deal with the conflict between rational actions and the emotional upheaval brought on by terrorism.

"Since 1959 the way in which the opposition has tried to stop the revolution was with tools of terrorism. Now go back to the dictator Batista—he repressed his enemies in practice but also repressed everyone else to create an atmosphere of fear. This phenomenon repeated itself after he was ousted and the revolution triumphed. The counter-revolutionaries were mostly those who had backed the Batista regime, and they used those same methods Batista did—terror—for the purpose of paralyzing the revolution and those who supported it.

"At the start of the revolution terrorism was supported and developed by a foreign government, the United States of America, which was also a world military power. In Cuba, the psychological point of view is that this terrorism is predominately external, it's not internal and that creates this deep sense of helplessness, of fear, and of a siege mentality.

And so the government creates policies to deal with the siege, they have to take steps to secure the nation and its people. Some of these policies are restrictive, and they are criticized for them. But it had to be done."

Terrorism against Cuba, Calviño notes, tries to accomplish something that is impossible.

"In order to understand the impact of terrorism you have to understand each person here is born with a Cuban identity. Our society, our psychological make-up is a result of our independence, which has created a Cuban national identity. This started from the wars in the nineteenth century for independence, to feel Cuban you were born with feelings of freedom, self-government. Fidel Castro's Revolution succeeded because it was made by Cubans for Cubans. Anything that now attempts to go against those feelings—such as terrorism—is an attempt to go against the Cuban identity. The only possible answer is to fight those who want to fight against the Cuban identity. And we can't fight against ourselves—we are who we are. So terrorism will never succeed because we would have to give up our Cuban identity first, and that will never happen. Remember, this is a home grown revolution, this has been made by Cubans, not imposed by outsiders."

Calviño switches to the importance of community as a weapon against terrorism.

"Terrorism, it's almost impossible to face alone. But when you have a network of people beside you, then the effect is different, not nearly as intense or damaging, because there is support. It's basic psychology—years ago when you went to the dentist it was usually just you and the dentist, and that created tremendous fear. Someone then realized if the patient was in a room with other people waiting for the dentist, then they would all be able to face their fear better.

"If we didn't have this network of support throughout the country how could the revolution have survived against the terrorist attacks? It is only through unity. Unity with differences, because there are 11 million people who live in Cuba, and we are all individuals. But unity and independence and the implacable right to do what we want to do, that is how we have survived. That sense of unity is intensified when everyone here knows our history against terrorism but no one outside Cuba does."

He recognizes that American policies have helped accelerate the development of *patria* (unity) within Cuba.

"I want the blockade lifted, but the United States government has no idea how they have helped the sense of *patria*, of surviving this siege through solidarity. So if the blockade ends will our sense of unity end? The end of the blockade will only mean one type of struggle will be over; but our effort to improve our society continues. The struggle to continue to build the society we wanted to build, to continue to develop our health care, our education, our ability to provide material goods, to advance the society the revolution wanted, will continue."

Calviño recounts an incident that he says, more than anything else, demonstrates the essence of the Cuban identity and why the revolution has survived.

"It was during my time on the *Contacto* show—one person called me and asked the relation between personality and astrology. I sarcastically answered back, I told her I'll answer from a psychologist's perspective. I said, what are you so worried about these stars in the sky millions of miles away? I'm not sure if stars have any influence on people, but between people there are more important things to consider, here and a lot closer than the stars.

"So I left the television studio and was driving home in my car. Another car pulled up beside me and a lady looked over and asked if I was that psychologist Calviño. I said yes, and she replied she was the one who asked the astrological question and that my answer was wrong. I told her I was not wrong. Then she asked me if I was a Leo, I said yes, I was, why ask? She said that's why you don't like to lose, because you're a Leo. I said yes I'm a Leo, I was born August 12. But that's not why I don't like to lose.

"I don't like to lose because I am Cuban."

14

The Cuban Five

Throughout the long war against terrorism the Cuban government has taken various measures in an attempt to protect its citizens and to end the attacks.

The terror has been basically two pronged. In the early years of the revolution from 1959 to the Bay of Pigs invasion of 1961 the actions in the majority were conducted by counter-revolutionaries inside Cuba. In reaction various internal policies were implemented. Measures such as the development of the Committee for Defense of the Revolution (CDR) were instituted to work as community watch programs in order for neighbors to spot and report any suspected terrorist activities. While the CDR often became politicized, the groups still operate today with the prime function still in place. Other strategies have resulted in certain restrictions of civil rights, particularly in regards to expressions of organized opposition perceived to be in the service of the American government. The Cuban side has determined unity to be a crucial weapon in combating terrorism, subsequently developing a low tolerance for anything that is seen to be jeopardizing strength of *patria*.

The second prong of the terrorist attacks has been the activities organized and conducted by anti-revolutionaries outside Cuba, most often based in Florida, more accurately centered in Miami.

To combat these organizations there has been only one choice—to send intelligence agents to penetrate the Cuban-American organizations in an attempt to gain information and warn the government of impending plots. Cuba has used these methods for almost as long as the terrorist war, increasingly so in the 1990s when they felt particularly vulnerable following the collapse of the Soviet Union. While the effectiveness of the program will not be known until all documents are made available, it is generally recognized the intelligence gathering has helped thwart dozens if not hundreds of acts.

The risk of that option comes if those sent to infiltrate are exposed. Which is what happened to the Cuban Five.

Gerardo Hernández, René González, Ramón Labañino, Antonio Guerrero and Fernando González were arrested, along with five other Cubans on June 8, 1998. The others pleaded guilty to charges related to their activities and served as witnesses against the Cuban Five. Those who plea bargained received light sentences and are now living freely in the United States.

The Cuban Five refused to admit to anything other than trying to gain information on possible terrorist acts being formulated by these Cuban-American groups. They were all charged with conspiracy to commit espionage, being unregistered agents for a foreign power and holding false documents. They were sentenced in September 2001 for a total of four life sentences and 75 years.

One of the Five, Gerardo Hernández, was additionally charged with conspiracy to commit murder. Gerardo's charge was based on the accusation that he was partially responsible for the death of the members of Brothers to the Rescue, whose planes were shot down by the Cuban air force. The Miami based counter-revolutionary group was picking up Cubans during the 1994 rafters crisis, but then turned to conducting illegal flights over Cuban airspace. After each incursion the government protested to the United States. Nothing was done to end the flights until two of the small planes were shot down—the Cubans claiming within their territorial jurisdiction, the American side saying they were downed over international waters. The intention of Brothers to the Rescue to violate Cuban airspace was well known in the Miami

Cuban community, as well as with Federal Aviation Administration officials. Gerardo, who was accused of warning the Cuban side of the flights, was given two life sentences plus 15 years. The defense argued that the activities of the Brothers was common knowledge to anyone connected with the Cuban community and that Gerardo was in no way responsible for what happened.[1]

Following the arrests the Five were put in solitary confinement for more than a year, and are now placed in separate penal institutions across America. Additionally, it has been extremely difficult for family members to visit the Five, with visas continually being denied.

In an ironic twist, the arrest of the Five was made possible partially from the substantial amount of information the Cuban Ministry of Interior gave to a delegation from the FBI on June 1998. The two sides were meeting to discuss terrorism following the series of hotel bombings, and at these sessions ministry officials handed over detailed accounts of actions and plans, recordings of phone conversations, videos, samples of explosive substances and other information their agents had gathered from infiltration work in Miami. The FBI officials thanked the Cubans, went back home and then used the material to uncover the agents.

The case has been challenged by the Cuban government and supporters as being unjust and corrupted by the influence of the exile community in Miami. A request to move the initial trial away from Miami was refused, and subsequent appeals were also rife with irregularities, according to legal experts.[2] During the trials a number of American military authorities, including General James Clapper, former head of the Intelligence Agency of the Defense Department, dismissed the possibility that any of the Five had access to secret documents or had compromised American national security. The prosecution never presented any documentary evidence to support the claim.

The case has attracted a great deal of international support, including from various Nobel Prize winners and heads of state. Websites such as the National Committee to Free the Cuban Five, www.freethefive. org, continue to champion their cause.

The Cuban government has long maintained the position that the Cuban Five had no intention to compromise any aspect of American national security—that their sole purpose was to prevent further terrorist attacks.

The United States 11th Circuit Court of Appeals in Atlanta seemed to support that view when it made note in its June 2008 ruling that it appeared there was no gathering or transmission of secret information affecting the national security of the United States.[3] The court went on to indicate that the only role of the Five was to penetrate terrorist groups in Miami. Additionally, there was no evidence to demonstrate the charge that any of the Five was directly involved in the deaths of the Brothers to the Rescue. In June 2009 the matter was sent to the United States Supreme Court, which refused to hear the case.

The Cuban Five is the only judicial proceeding in United States history condemned by the Work Group of Arbitrary Detention of the United Nations Commission on Human Rights. The panel stated in 2005 that the trial was not impartial and the sentences were excessively severe.

OLGA SALANUEVA AND ELIZABETH PALMEIRO

Both Olga Salanueva and Elizabeth Palmeiro continue to hold out hope that their husbands will one day return to Cuba.

Of the Five, Olga's husband René González is closest to release. He may be free in 2013, sooner if there is any consideration for time off for good behavior.

Ramón Labañino, received a life sentence plus 18 years. At the time of the interview in June 2009 he was one of the three planned to be re-sentenced in Florida in October 2009, under the direction of the Atlanta appeals court. "I don't know what will happen, but I don't have much hope," Ramón's wife Elizabeth admitted.

As for "the fifth" Gerardo, Elizabeth commented sadly, "He has two life sentences; the legal process is over for Gerardo. American justice has decided he has to die in prison, unless there is another solution."

Both wives stressed that as far as they are concerned, after the latest development from the Supreme Court, the proof is overwhelming that this was never about justice, but politics.

Olga Salanueva and
Elizabeth Palmeiro

"The normal sentence in these matters is five or ten years," Olga says. "If the Five were not Cuban this would not have happened. I'm totally convinced of that. Why were the Cuban Five given so much? The length of these sentences is so unjust. For what, to try and protect the Cuban people from terrorism? They never at any time had anything to do with American national security."

From the moment the request to move the trial from Miami was denied, "It was clear they would never get a fair trial there, with so much pressure on the judge and jury from the anti-Castro Cuban-Americans. The media immediately called them spies, demanding long sentences. Moving the trial away from Miami was the basic thing to do. Once that was not done it was so obvious that the trial would be biased, that their fate was determined," Elizabeth commented.

Like almost all aspects of the contentious relationship between Cuba and America, the Five are seen in black and white terms. In Cuba they are considered heroes—and the government expends a large amount of time and energy trying to secure their release. For the other side, the Five are spies.

Olga and Elizabeth see their husbands as simply trying to help prevent further acts of terrorism, to save the lives of innocents.

"They were there to infiltrate the groups that have committed acts of terrorism against Cuba. They never had access to sensitive documents, they had no intent to compromise American government secrets. All they wanted to do was infiltrate these organizations in order to prevent further attacks," Olga says.

"Terrorism against Cuba is older than we are," 44-year-old Elizabeth continues. "So we've been born and raised knowing about terrorism against Cuba and knowing friends who lost their children, when bombs were put in stores, nurseries, the Cubana Airlines. So for Cubans living here it's not difficult to know about terrorism. When you know the history of terrorism against us, you have to do anything to stop it. If not for the terrorism, there would be no need for the Cuban Five.

"Historically, in the first months of the revolution there were people who left Cuba, those most affected negatively. They took away money. They also took away all their hate and found support in the United States government for a long time. They were armed and financed by the US government and they have taken so many actions against Cuba.

"If it is not possible to reach agreement between us and these counter-revolutionary groups, then in some way Cubans have to be warned so we can avoid these acts of terrorism. We can't stop them all but whatever can be done should be done."

As far as Olga in concerned, "We had no choice but to prevent these acts by sending men for the sake of our country and family. They left their families behind to prevent these actions and to try and avoid more deaths. We couldn't invade Florida, like America did to Afghanistan.

The way the Americans have waged their war against terrorism, we can't do it that way."

Both wives then turn to how difficult it has been to see their husbands in jail.

"René gets approved visits each weekend, relatives included. The only relatives he has are in Cuba. So we need a visa to visit the United States. That has been used as a tool for additional torture, getting these visas is very difficult. In ten years these visas have been issued only a few times," Olga states.

"Gerardo has never been able to see his wife, Adrianna. She received one visa in 2002, went to the United States and they stopped her, then ordered her to return to Cuba. It's absurd, ever since then they've denied any visa for her," Elizabeth relates.

The last time Elizabeth saw Ramón, who is in a facility in Kentucky, was October 2008. While it appears the judicial avenue for the Five has all but ended, Olga and Elizabeth express confidence that justice can be achieved through the increased amount of awareness the case is engendering internationally.

"The Cuban government and international groups are continuing the campaign to free the Five," Elizabeth says. "We need as much support as we can get, anything that can be done is vital. The families of the Five are at the head of the campaign, and it helps give us strength to continue. Many solidarity communities have been formed for the Cuban Five."

The difficulty, Olga admits, is to inform the American public first about the history of terrorism against Cuba, so they can understand why the Cuban Five were needed.

"The American population doesn't know about this history of terrorism, so how can they connect this with the Cuban Five? You have to understand how many acts of terrorism have been committed against Cuba, only then you can realize why the Cuban Five did what they had to. But the judge in Miami didn't want this history to be used as a motive. It was the only motive, there was nothing else. Without allowing that how could anyone understand why the Cuban Five were there?

"So now, if the judicial process is over we have to work on the solidarity of public opinion, to put pressure on the US government. This has never been about the legal system, it's all about politics, so maybe that's the way it will be solved."

On a personal level, the two admit it is a daily struggle.

Elizabeth comments, "I don't know how to survive this day to day, it is hard. But we have so much support in Cuba, and with others around the world. This is a unifying factor in Cuba now, everyone knows about the situation and it helps in our struggle. We just need more and more people to be aware about this."

Knowing their husbands remain in jail "gives us determination. We have no choice but to continue. They are not tired in prison, we can not be tired. We are enduring pain and suffering but others have endured worse, they have had their fathers, mothers, sons and daughters killed by terrorists. Thousands of Cubans have been killed. We need many like the Cuban Five, as we are all exposed to terrorism. I don't know, but I'm sure there are more Cuban agents trying to do the same work as the Cuban Five, to infiltrate these terrorist organizations. They are still needed."

Each wife was asked what they would say to their husband if he walked through the door.

"If René came through the door right now, I'd grab his hand and say let's go and take a walk."

"If Ramón walked through, I'd tell him don't you dare go anywhere again."

Notes

CHAPTER 1   THE UNKNOWN WAR

1. Ann Louise Bardach and Larry Rohter, "A Cuban Exile Details Horrendous Matter of a Bombing Campaign," *NY Times*, July 12, 1998, pp. 10–11.
2. April 28, 1823 in US Congress, House of Reps, Island of Cuba, p. 7.
3. *Congressional Globe*, February 17, 1859, 35th Congress, 2nd session, vol. 36, pt. 1, pp. 1080–1.
4. William H. Mills, *The Purpose of the Nation in the Present War*, San Francisco, 1898, pp. 25, 36–7.
5. Emily S. Rosenberg, "Rescuing Women and Children," in Joanne Meyerwitz (ed.), *History and September 11*, Philadelphia, 2003, pp. 83–5. Louis A. Pérez Jr., *Cuba in the American Imagination*, University of North Carolina Press, Chapel Hill, 2008, p. 73.
6. *Philadelphia Manufacturer*, March 15, 1889, p. 3.
7. *Brooklyn Eagle*, August 23, 1902, p. 4.
8. "Down at Last," *New York World*, June 14, 1901.
9. One of the many promotions to convince Americans to come and colonize Cuba was an 1899 advertising poster by The Cuban Colonization Company which was titled (in part) "Fortunes in Cuba – A short road to a competency and a life amid tropical delights for those who are awake to the present opportunity. Owns and holds deeds for two large tracts of the best land in Cuba..." Reprinted from Enrique Cirules, *Conversacion con el ultimo northamericano*, Editorial Letra Cubanas, Habana, 1988.
10. Albert J. Beveridge, "Cuba and Congress," *North American Review* 62, July 1901. Pérez, *Cuba in the American Imagination*, p. 19.
11. *New York Post*, July 21, 1898, p. 2.
12. *Six Crises*, Garden City, New York, 1962, p. 352, p. 20.
13. Barry Goldwater, *Why Not Victory*, New York, 1962, p. 78.

14. Richard Welch, *Response to Revolution: The United States and the Cuban Revolution, 1951–1961*, Chapel Hill, 1985, p. 186.

15. Barry Goldwater, *Vital Speeches*, p. 422, cited in Pérez, *Cuba in the American Imagination*, p. 247.

16. Congressional Record, January 25, 1960, 86th Congress, 2nd session. June 25, vol. 106, pt. 2, p. 14385.

17. The policy began shortly after the revolution and continues to this day. In 1992 Democrat Robert Torricelli commented, a year after Congress passed the embargo-tightening act that carried his name, "I want to wreck havoc on that island." Lars Schoultz, *That Infernal Little Cuban Republic*, University of North Carolina Press, 2009.

    In 2000 the bi-partisan nature of the policy was once again revealed when Republican whip Tom Delay said, in response to why the embargo hasn't worked, "Because we have not been turning the screws on him (Castro) and screwing him down and putting pressure on him, so that the people will rise up and throw him out." Louis A. Pérez Jr., *Cuba Between Reform and Revolution*, third edition, Oxford University Press, New York, 2006, p. 313.

18. Don Bohning, *The Castro Obsession*, Potomac Books, 2005. Cuba uses historical examples (Britain as one) of a country acting undemocratically in times of war or threats to national security to defend itself. Historically, nations under terrorist attack have moved to restrict certain civil liberties in an attempt to protect themselves from internal and external dangers—the Patriot Act is one of the latest cases.

19. House Select Committee on Assassinations Report, Vol. IV, p. 125. September 22, 1978.

20. Noam Chomsky, *Z Magazine*, February 2005, p. 43.

21. Cuban National Assembly President Ricardo Alarcon admitted the siege has taken a toll: "It has cost us millions in resources, diverted attention and efforts to help make sure our people are safe from terrorist attacks, and made it harder for us in our plans to trade internationally. The terrorist attacks, unknown outside Cuba, have hurt us the greatest; physically, socially and emotionally. And it is the most frustrating because no one knows. So how are we to protect ourselves?" Interview with author, August 2007.

22. American policy aim remains regime change through internal unrest. In the 1990s, the Torricelli Act and Helms-Burton Act were passed to tighten the economic screws on Cuba following the collapse of the Soviet Union. The most direct example of this is the 2004 Commission for Assistance to a Free Cuba, a cabinet-level directive. The Commission report outlined the intention

to play a large role in post-Castro Cuba. It is the blueprint for America's re-integration into all aspects of Cuban life. The Cubans view it as proof of US desire to re-impose hegemony.

23. Fidel Castro during annual July 26, 1993 speech in Santiago.

24. Warren Hinckle and William Turner, *The Fish is Red*, Harper and Row, New York, 1981, p. 293.

25. Arocena's testimony came during his trial for terrorist acts against Miami targets. Despite the confession he was never charged for his part in biological warfare. Federal Tribunal of the City of New York, p. 2189, 1984, exp. FBI NY 185-1009.

CHAPTER 2   CUBANA AIRLINES

1. Posada's admitted involvement in the bombings came in a *NY Times* article. Ann Louise Bardach and Larry Rohter, "A Cuban Exile Details Horrendous Matter of a Bombing Campaign," *NY Times*, July 12, 1998, pp 10–11. He later recanted his statements.

2. On the attempt and pardon: http://news.bbc.co.uk/2/hi/americas/3603682. stm. On the pardon being ruled unconstitutional: http://www.reuters.com/article/worldNews/idUSN0119961420080701.

3. National Security Archives, The Posada Files, http://www.gwu.edu/~nsarchiv/NSAEBB/NSAEBB157/index.htm.

4. Ann Louise Bardach, "Twilight of the Assassins," *The Atlantic*, November 2006. The article also reports that in 1982 another Cuban, Ricardo "El Mono" Morales, claimed responsibility for the bombing in a confession videotaped by Posada's attorney. El Mono was a known CIA and FBI informant, involved in drugs and notoriously unreliable. Shortly after his confession he was killed gangland-style by a drug thug. Posada's lawyer was killed a year later.

5. "Bosch Denounces US Report on Terrorist Activities," *Miami Herald*, August 5, 1989. As part of the move to deport Bosch, the Department of Justice Associate Attorney General reported: "Information reflecting that the October 6, 1976 Cuban airline bombing was a CORU operation under the direction of Bosch," National Security Archives, Posada File.

CHAPTER 3   HOTEL BOMBINGS

1. John Kirk, *Globe & Mail*, October 11, 1993.

2. Weekly News Update on the Americas, #218, April 3, 1994.

3. Ann Louise Bardach and Larry Rohter, "Key Cuba Foe Claims Exile's Backing," *NY Times*, July 12, 1998, p. 10.
4. Ibid.
5. The January 1999 UN report, under the Economic and Social Council, detailed the invitation to visit Havana to interview those connected with the bombings: http://www.unhchr.ch/Huridocda/Huridoca.nsf/0811fcbd0b9f6b d58025667300306dea/ab78acfb0828505780256737003f82a4. Following the special rapporteur's visit in September, the Council released his extensive findings two months later: http://www.unhchr.ch/Huridocda/Huridoca.nsf/0 /0c9e82b68055b832802568960059e1d5/$FILE/G9916486.pdf, p. 10.
6. Jim DeFede, *Havana Journal*, August 6, 2005. DeFede is a former *Miami Herald* columnist.
7. Bardach and Rohter, "Key Cuba Foe Claims Exile's Backing."
8. Ibid.

CHAPTER 4   OPERATION PETER PAN

1. Juan Carlos Rodriquez, *The Bay of Pigs and the CIA*, Ocean Press, Melbourne, 1999.
2. Interview with Ramón Torreira, co-author of *Operación Peter Pan*, Editoria Politica, Havana, 2000. He doubts the story is true.
3. Yvonne M. Conde, *Operacion Pedro Pan*, Routledge, New York, 1999. "30 Years Later, Pedro Pan Children Recalled," *Miami Herald*, November 24, 1990.
4. Rodriquez, *The Bay of Pigs and the CIA*. Ramón Torreira Crespo and José Buajasan Marrawi, *Operación Peter Pan*, Editoria Politica, Havana, 2000. Maria de los Angeles Torres, "The CIA, National Security and Pedro Pan," *Miami Herald*, December 18, 1994.
5. Sergio Lopez-Miro, "The Dark Side of Peter Pan," *Miami Herald*, November 29, 1990.

CHAPTER 5   BIOLOGICAL TERRORISM

1. Warren Hinckle and William Turner, *The Fish is Red*, Harper & Row, New York, 1981.
2. Bill Schaap, "The 1981 Cuba Dengue Epidemic," *Covert Action* 17, 1982.
3. Hinckle and Turner, *The Fish is Red*.

4. Lars Schoultz, *That Infernal Little Cuban Republic*, University of North Carolina Press, 2009, pp. 178, 189. Operation Mongoose was part of the terror program developed by the US after the Bay of Pigs failure.

5. Ariel Alonso Pérez, *Biological Warfare against Cuba*, Capitan San Luis, Havana, 2008.

6. Ibid.

7. Federal Tribunal of the City of New York, p. 2189, 1984, exp. FBI NY 185-1009.

8. Jane Franklin, Z *Magazine*, June 2003.

9. Peréz, *Biological Warfare against Cuba*.

10. Unfortunately Robaina passed away at the age of 91 on April 17, 2010.

CHAPTER 6   BOCA DE SAMÁ

1. A *Miami New Times* article August 6, 2009 by Tim Elfrink, "He Buried Che," revealed details of Cuban-American Gustavo Villodo's involvement in organizing the attack. The article claimed Villodo co-ordinated the assault with an old CIA contact in Washington. Villodo is a long time anti-revolutionary connected with many violent Miami-based groups, also involved in Che's death in Bolivia.

2. www.alpha66.org.

3. The attack on the Moncada military garrison July 26, 1953 by Fidel Castro and his supporters is one of the defining moments of the revolution. The attack failed, Castro was arrested, and it was in his subsequent trial that he gave his "History Will Absolve Me" speech. The event, which gave the name to Castro's revolutionary movement (Movimiento 26 Julio), is still commemorated annually.

CHAPTER 8   LITERACY CAMPAIGN

1. *Cuba: The Untold History*, Editorial Capitan San Luis, Havana, 2005.

CHAPTER 10   LA COUBRE

1. Jane Franklin, *Cuba and the United States*, Ocean Press, Melbourne, 1997, p. 23. Throughout the early years up to the Bay of Pigs invasion the Americans tried to stop other countries from selling arms to Cuba. The Cubans turned to the Soviets for armaments, a situation the Americans then utilized as proof of the communist nature of the Castro regime.

2. *Cuba: The Untold History*, Editorial Capitan San Luis, Havana, 2005.
3. Fabian Escalante, *The Cuba Project*, Ocean Press, Melbourne, 2004.
4. Navil Garcia Alfonso, "Washington Maintains Strict Silence over the Sabotage of the French Boat," Granma International, March 15, 2006.

CHAPTER 11   DEPARTMENT STORES

1. The CIA is implicated in both. The Veciana connection is described in Julia E. Sweig, *Cuba: What Everyone Needs to Know*, Oxford University Press, 2009, p. 49. The MRP was linked to the CIA through advisor Jorge Comellas, an agent trained in terrorist activities. Juan Carlos Rodriquez, *The Bay of Pigs and the CIA*, Ocean Press, Melbourne, 1999, p. 29.

CHAPTER 13   THE CUBAN NATIONAL IDENTITY

1. Louis A. Pérez Jr., *Cuba Between Reform and Revolution*, third edition, Oxford University Press, New York, 2006, p. 328.
2. The 1933 revolution overthrew American supported President Gerardo Machado and led to movement towards political reform and a series of social justice programs, including nationalizing US properties. The revolt and its aftermath were short lived, thanks in part to US opposition to the new policies. Emerging as the man in control of a re-established government compliant to American approval, under President Ramon Grau San Martin, was a then unknown military officer, Fulgencio Batista.
3. In the first years of the revolution a number of mass organizations were formed; for education, youth, community projects, and national defense. It was a method to engender revolutionary spirit among the people years before the one-party state was institutionalized. The CDR was set up in September 1960 specifically to help identify potential anti-revolutionary sympathizers prior to the expected invasion of Cuba, which happened at the Bay of Pigs in April 1961. Besides a watch for fifth columnists, the CDR helped identify criminal activity, assisted in labor mobilization, supported attendance at political rallies and even kept neighborhoods clean. It has also been subject to social and political abuses where incidents of spreading gossip and unjustified accusations have occurred. The political aspects of the CDR have considerably lessened now, although it still serves a social and security purpose.
4. The three hurricanes that hit Cuba in 2008 were Gustav, Ike, and Paloma. The storms caused an estimated $2 billion in damages, destroying thousands

of homes. The country continues to recover from the devastation, particularly the agricultural losses.

5. America entered Cuba's war of independence against Spain in 1898, resulting in America's virtual control over the country's economic and political systems until 1959.

6. After the fall of the Soviet Union in 1989 when Cuba experienced tremendous economic loss and entered into its Special Period, America passed the Torricelli and Helms-Burton acts. Both acts were designed to tighten the embargo, such as making it illegal for US subsidiaries to trade with Cuba, as well as setting out all aspects of a post-Castro regime, including who the Cubans could elect as president.

CHAPTER 14   THE CUBAN FIVE

1. Background on the flights is extensive, including: Barbara Crossette, "UN Wont Punish Cuba in Downing of Planes," NY *Times*, July 27, 1996; http://www.themilitant.com/2009/7329/732950.html or for the United Nations report at http://www.un.org/en/sc/repertoire/96-99/CHAPTER 8/ Americas/19-shooting down of aircraft.pdf.

2. Michael Steven Smith, "A Tale of Two Lawsuits," in Salim Lamrani (ed.), *Superpower Principles: U.S. Terrorism against Cuba*, Common Courage Press, Monroe, ME, 2005.

3. On June 4, 2008 the three-judge, 11th Circuit Court panel vacated the life sentences of René Gonzalez and Guerrero as well as Fernando Gonzalez's 19-year sentence, concurring with their argument that their sentences were improperly configured because they did not gather or transmit classified information. The three were ordered to be re-sentenced. On September 2, 2008 the court denied a defense appeals request to re-hear. Both actions can be found at www.freethefive.org.

Index